DO YOU REALLY BELIEVE THAT?

The thoughts and views of an ordinary atheist

Paul Davis-Cooke

ISBN-13: 9798848361148
ISBN-10: 1477123456

Cover design by: Art Painter
Library of Congress Control Number: 2018675309
Printed in the United States of America

*This book is dedicated to all those who seek
answers through increased knowledge and to those
who prize honest inquiry above dogma.*

CONTENTS

PREFACE

As a life long non-believer, at least all my adult life, I have nonetheless always been fascinated by the twin the subjects of God and religion. I have read the holy books of the Abrahamic faiths many times and I have a lesser familiarity with the offerings of other religions.

Over the past few years, I have amused myself by writing small essays on religious belief in general and the Abrahamic faiths in particular; a few have even been published as articles in atheist magazines.

During the, near terminal, boredom of the recent Covid 19 lockdown, a friend proposed the idea of collecting a few of these personal musings into a volume and so, being a highly suggestable creature of ego, I did.

INTRODUCTION

My story and how not to behave as an atheist

Do you usually read the intro? I don't. I sometimes go back and read it later but often they are boring and too long. Please give this one a try. It's not too long, I hope it's not boring and it will set up the rest of the book. I promise.

What you are about to delve into is simply a collection of short essays I have written, over a few years. Some were written for publication in magazines, some were just my way of sorting out my thoughts. I do not claim anything here is original or unique and the more well-read of you will recognise ideas already put forward by others, almost certainly better than I do here. So, why publish? I suppose I hope that putting my thoughts in print may, in some small way, help others to form their own opinions on certain topics. And hey, a new car would be nice.

I want to begin by saying that, despite the sub-heading, I'm not going to preach to you about how to behave. You're an adult and you make your own choices. What I will do is tell you a little about me and I'll make a couple of suggestions about interacting with religious people, that I hope will be interesting and possibly helpful.
Right, let's get on with it.

Once I had decided to write this book and knowing I needed an intro, I could think of nothing more appropriate than a brief account of how I became convinced that God does not exist. Along the way I want to define a few words, so that my meaning will be understood later. Perhaps I should start with the big one.

The observant reader will notice that I capitalised the word God. I do this solely because it is a title and not because I write this in a nominally Christian country (England) and from a background firmly fixed in what is commonly called the Judaeo-Christian tradition. Throughout the book, I will refer to the monotheistic god of the three Abrahamic faiths, Judaism, Christianity and Islam, as God. I presume that my disbelief in any other deity or pantheon is understood.

I should also clarify at this point that what follows is solely about those three religions. I do not address Hinduism or any other faith and for good reason. I was raised in the West and my knowledge of other religions is insufficient to allow for any meaningful criticism.

Another definition I believe essential is that of Atheist. Open any English dictionary and you will find something similar to the following: *'a person who believes that God does not exist'*. This is fine as far as it goes but it is a little too specific regarding belief and it begs the question, which god? I have partly answered this above but it needs to be pinned down a little more.

Belief in the Abrahamic God is called Theism. That is, belief in a god which interacts with his creation and with mankind. This is very different from Deism, which is a belief in a divine creator of the universe but one which does not interact with it, in any noticeable way.

It is today widely accepted that the Founding Fathers of the USA were all Deists. They understood the power of religion and made it clear that government had no business interfering. It is concomitant that religion should have no place in politics either, something modern America would do well to keep in mind. But I digress.

As mentioned, the dictionary definition given above is too simplistic. To many atheists, their position is not one of a positive statement regarding the non-existence of God but rather a lack of belief based on insufficient evidence, some may say on no evidence whatsoever.

So, despite what some religious apologists would have their followers believe, being an atheist does not mean you hate God, nor is it a religion itself. Atheists range from a simple lack of belief to actively asserting there is no God. More of that later.

That's enough dry academic stuff for now. Let me tell you about how I became an atheist and how I moved passed it.

From my present-day perspective, I can see that I was wise in my choice of parents and my country of birth. Had I not shown foresight rare in the unborn, I may have come into the world in a very different situation. I may have been born to observant Muslims in an Islamic country, or to evangelical Christians in the Bible Belt of America. Either way, and in a host of other similar possibilities, I would almost certainly have been brought up strictly according to the faith of my parents and imbued with the faith driven culture in which they lived. Had such been the case, it is extremely unlikely that I would be writing this.

My parents were nominally Christian and, if pressed, they would have described themselves as Church of England. The English church began as a way of allowing a king to divorce and remarry. It adopted Protestantism, not from conviction but merely to conveniently separate it from Papal rule. It went through many years of conflict with Catholicism and struggled with Puritanism, but today it is more like a social club than a religion. There is little of the fervour shown by other Christian sects or indeed other religions. That is not to say that C of E followers are not serious about God but only that, in typical British fashion, they prefer not to be terribly strident about it. Indeed, many British people tend to look upon outward displays of emotion with some discomfort.

So it was that I grew up knowing I was a Christian and, irregularly, attending Sunday school, but understanding that my faith was a private thing, only to be brought out on Sundays or at weddings, Christenings and funerals, where I sang hymns with gusto. It was never to be discussed with strangers or preached about and it was not to form an active part of my daily life, lest I be led into the sin of pride and proselytising, like the Catholics. There is an old adage that there are three things never to be discussed in a pub; politics, football and religion.

This lack of passion in matters of religion made it easier for me to handle a change which occurred when I was in my teens. Like many young people I was looking for a sense of identity. I flirted with gangs but I was never truly convinced that being a skinhead, a biker or a hippy, was the answer to life's ineffable mysteries (and yet, embarrassingly, I tried two of them. Growing my hair from schoolboy skinhead to hippy took so long, I had finished college before I looked convincing and then I had to get it cut to start my first job. I only avoided being a biker because I couldn't afford a Chopper).

And then, during a brief venture into genealogy, I discovered a minor Jewish heritage in my family tree. It mattered not to me that Jews place emphasis on the matriarchal line and that it was someone in my Father's family who had been Jewish, nor did it matter that this ethnicity was never confirmed through geneology; suddenly, I was a Jew. It was something I could be proud of. Different enough to be radical, for a working-class teenager in middle England, with an added frisson of danger due to the Arab-Israeli conflict and with the right to display my righteous indignation at the Holocaust, at length, should anyone care to listen. And I really wanted people to listen.

I embraced Judaism with the passion of a convert, much to my parent's displeasure. They had nothing against Jews but they had lived through the Second World War and had witnessed anti-Semitism, before I even knew the word, and they did not want their son suffering such treatment over what they hoped would be a short-lived teenaged phase.

I purchased a copy of the Tanakh, the Christian Old Testament but with the books in their original order, before the church of Rome decided it knew best. I had a Torah, the first five books of Moses and I even, very briefly, dipped into the Babylonian Talmud, the immense volumes of commentary and discussion based on study of the Torah and designed to answer questions about how what was written should be applied to day-to-day issues. I wore a skull cap and a prayer shawl on the Sabbath and I even nailed the Mezzuzah to the frame of our front door, for which my Father was grateful, of course. For those who don't know, the Mezzuzah is a small metal container which holds a tiny scroll bearing a Hebrew prayer, "Hear, O Israel, the Lord is our God, the Lord is one. You shall love the Lord, your God, with all your heart, with all your soul, and with all your resources......" It goes on a bit but you don't want the whole thing.

I began to learn Hebrew, which did not go well and I met regularly with a Rabbi, with whom I discussed my intention to convert and who, as he was obliged to do, tried to talk me out of it. Although orthodox Jews do not accept converts, Reform and Modern Jews do, but they make it difficult, in order to discourage anyone with any uncertainty. I was not discouraged and I eventually undertook the full immersion baptism to make me a Jew. It was only a short time later that my life took another unexpected turn.

My first job was in local government as an administrator and after a few years I had been promised a promotion, as a reward for overseeing the computerisation of my section without an increase in pay. When the task was completed, the role of department head was given to the area manager's secretary/ girlfriend and, with the fire of youth in my belly, I marched into his office, spoke pompously of favouritism and injustice and told him right where he could shove his job. Then I went home, cooled down and realised that I was unemployed. To make matters worse, because I had resigned voluntarily, I was not entitled to state benefits. As loving as my parent were, I understood that living off them was not going to be an option, especially after damaging a perfectly good door frame with my little religious symbol.

Later that day, whilst glancing through the Situations Vacant column of the newspaper, I came across something that immediately interested me and filled me with a real sense of God's purpose (it's embarrassing to admit). It was an advertisement for young people to come and work and live on a Kibbutz in Israel. I didn't even have to think about it. I applied and shortly thereafter was accepted. Only then did I tell my parents.

As you may imagine, there was much wailing and gnashing of teeth but I would not be dissuaded. A month later I was on a plane headed for the promised land.

This is not the place to go into depth about my, very short, time in Israel but I do need to relate one of the most important things I encountered and how it changed my life completely. I had arrived thinking that my discovery of a Jewish heritage, my conversion, the heated end of my employment and the advert for new Kibbutzim were all meant to be and that I was part of something bigger. Would it be arrogant to say divine plan? Well yes, of course it would but I was still naïve. What I did not expect and what initially shocked me, was that virtually no-one on the kibbutz was religious. To them, being Jewish was much more than a religion. It was a history, a culture, a shared experience and, in Zionism, a political movement dedicated to growing the Jewish homeland. They had no time for religious zeal; they were all too busy trying to stay alive.

I didn't know what to make of the attitude of the Sabra's, (native born Israelis, named after a local fruit with a soft sweet core protected by a hard outer skin). I was irritated by their good-natured ribbing of my beliefs and I was confused. As the days went by, I too became bound up with the harsh realities of life on a communal farm only yards from the border with Syria and my religious convictions began to waver. I remember wondering how Jews, a people actually living their faith and so different from the church of my childhood, could be so pragmatic and even careless about their relationship with God. I began to question.

Life on the kibbutz was not the glorious adventure expected by a young man with foolish ideas about himself and the world and I was soon home again. But still wondering about the conundrum of religious observance. Strangely, it was my deep conviction that Judaism was the way, that ultimately led to me replacing faith with reason.

I had read my Bible as a child and my Torah as a teen but now, in my early twenties, I read with a more critical eye. And I saw so much inconsistency and so much which I struggled to accept. I sought out books on biblical study and interpretation in order to shore up my beliefs and I found them unconvincing. I read authors with a totally opposite view and, slowly, they began to make sense.

The philosopher Bertrand Russell's book, 'Why I'm not a Christian' had a huge impact on me. I later saw him interviewed on TV and his succinct answer to the key question has stayed with me.

"Because I see no evidence whatever for any of the Christian dogmas. I have examined all the stock arguments for the existence of God and none of them seem to me to be logically valid".

That appeal to logic is what really fascinated me. Despite not being particularly assiduous in my schoolwork, as an adult I have always enjoyed learning and I developed logical, critical thinking quite naturally. Something else Russell said in the same interview neatly described my own experience.

"I never decided that I didn't want to remain a believer".

Like Russell, I never made a conscious choice. The more I read and the more critical my thinking, the more it became impossible for me to continue believing something which was incongruous with what I knew of the world and was clearly unsupported by evidence. I finally saw that the holy books of Judaism and Christianity were works of faith, not fact. Myth and legend woven into an account of more recent people and places to make the whole thing seem like history. At this point I was unable to dispute with believers but I knew I could no longer hold to something I now viewed as man-made fiction.

So, I was now a non-believer. At first, I was more agnostic than atheist, but that was really only down to me being uncomfortable with finally turning my back on something which had been so integral to my life. Over the next few years, I read more and more material from both sides of the argument and my stance finally became entrenched, not just as an atheist but as an anti-theist. Not only did I not believe, I was also appalled at what God supposedly did, condoned and ordered done. It was from this position that I became (drum roll please) a militant atheist.

With the passion I had once devoted to religion, I became an activist in what I saw as the fight against the evils of religion. I missed no opportunity to argue my case, nor was I kind or even polite in my methods. Looking back now, I am ashamed of my behaviour. I had been raised to be respectful of everyone unless and until they proved themselves unworthy. Sad to say, I saw believers as, at best, fools and, at worst, liars and manipulators. Thankfully, I eventually matured and moved beyond this unpleasantness.

As the years passed, I mellowed. I came to see that believers were, in the main, good people who were as convinced of their position as I was of mine. Moreover, I had to admit that I could no more prove that God did not exist than they could prove he did. I continued to campaign but I did so in a gentle fashion and I withheld my vitriol for those who clearly abused their position, such as paedophile priests, the Roman church telling Africans in danger of contracting HIV that condoms were evil, Catholic priests in Rwanda who called for genocide from the pulpit and Imams who call for Jihad. There are so many other examples.
I found that reading Christopher Hitchens, Richard Dawkins,

Daniel Dennett, Sam Harris and others reinforced my intellectual understanding of the arguments whilst easing me away from the need to fight every battle.

Today I think very differently. For one thing, I no longer call myself an atheist. The concept is not mine but I decided I did not wish to be defined by a negative. There are many things I don't believe in but I do not feel it necessary to describe myself in terms of what I do not believe. Instead, I have adopted Humanism. Without God as an excuse, a crutch or a scapegoat, it falls to us to be responsible for our actions and our inaction, in terms of man's inhumanity to man, how we treat the planet and our relationship with the myriad forms of life with whom we share it. I should be clear that my humanism is not elitist. It does not place mankind above everything else, it only removes the need for a god to dictate to me.

I now look back down the telescope of my own life and see an evolution in my thinking. I cannot say whether where I am now is where I will remain, but I am comfortable that I am able to discuss religion and faith objectively, calmly and with a fair degree of knowledge. I am better able to formulate my arguments without descending into disrespect and insult and without belittling those who believe. Indeed, I find it strange that so many atheists are easily led into unattractive diatribe and poor behaviour. I am more inclined to accept it from believers, who often feel their very personal relationship with God is threatened and who respond to that threat emotionally. But many atheists consider themselves to be enlightened. They are supposed to be the ones who see more clearly. How then can such people justify speaking insults and being, at times, deeply unpleasant?

I would like to ask all non-believers to be civil; to hold the moral high ground, to use logic and calm intellectual argument rather than anger or insults and to allow reason to triumph over superstition by force of argument and not by force of personality. It doesn't matter that you are right, if you seek to win a battle by beating down your opponent, you are wasting your time. Would *you* respond favourably to someone doing that to you? Would *you* listen?

I do not consider non-believers to be better than their religious counterparts but I do think that our thoughts and deliberations are less clouded by dogma and proscriptive rules. As such, I think we are better able to see clearly. This being so, isn't it is our responsibility to help others? To facilitate their journey towards understanding that what they have been told is truth is, in reality, merely belief. Faith, not fact. To help them understand that beliefs, no matter how deeply held and sincere, may be wrong.

If we discuss religion with the religious, we should not go for the throat. It will never be accepted and the recipient of your infallible logic, your clarity of thought, your education and all-round brilliance, will either turn away or get angry. And you have lost. Instead, try to find some common ground, ask questions, clarify their real position, not what you think it is. And then ask that they consider something small. Something that doesn't immediately set off their alarm but which might be a tiny crack in the dam, that grows slowly until the refreshing waters of the Enlightenment burst forth.

OK, sermon over. Let's get on with it.

Although the rest of this book is not in chronological order, this first offering is from an earlier time. In tone it is a little acerbic but I think it still expresses my overall opinion quite well.

INCREDULOUS & UNBELIEVING

We are expected to believe that God created this whole cosmos. A universe which, whilst not infinite, is so huge that the imagination cannot grasp it. The vast majority of this immensity is not only unaware of our existence it is actually incredibly harmful to life in general.

God supposedly created this unimaginably huge, largely empty, wholly inhospitable marvel simply to have a personal relationship with one species of primate that can only exist in certain limited regions of a planet orbiting a small star on the outer rim of one middling sized galaxy among billions. And, very strangely, after creating this utterly incredible and wondrous universe and everything in it, this god seems to be obsessively concerned with what we wear, what food we eat and, as has been noted before, what we do while naked.

God, it seems, created gravity. He created the strong nuclear force and the weak nuclear force. He created stars, black holes and dark matter. Unless you believe the Bible to be literally true, he also created all the stars but gave them a limited life, so that they would explode and give birth to all the heavier elements, which could then be combined in such a way as to give rise to everything material we see around us and all the life that has evolved over millennia. He must have been a bit tired after that because he left mankind alone for thousands of years, to struggle in brutish ignorance.

The Bible, of course, states that God created the Earth before the rest of the universe and that he lit it before he had set the sun and moon to orbit around the Earth, just underneath all the water that surrounds us in space. But we'll get to the rest of that nonsense later.

After billions of years, or six days and presumably well rested, he then revealed himself, not to mankind in general but to poor illiterate peasants in a remote part of the middle east. This made his very existence difficult for other people to accept. He also revealed himself to different people in different ways and demanded different things of them, including instructions to various groups that everyone else was wrong and must be made to 'see the light' and this caused thousands of years of suffering. He revealed himself in order to tell us that homosexuality is wrong but slavery is fine, we should love everyone but kill those who don't believe as we do and we must butcher the genitalia of our babies and young women and never forget that women are subservient to men in all things.

To begin with he wanted us to worship him by burning animals, so that he could enjoy the smell, but later he went off this idea. At one point he got so angry with us that he wiped out all life on Earth, except for one family and representatives of every species of animal (and presumably plants too, although this isn't mentioned in his book). After that, he suspended his law about incest so that his favoured family could repopulate the planet.

For reasons known only to himself, God chose not to communicate his greatness and his instructions to people in China, who were already highly literate and were plotting the paths of stars, but only to a chap named Abram, who was told to move home and change his name, so he could be the father of a chosen people who would teach the rest of us all about God.

Because of this decision, his 'favourites' suffered untold misery, war and persecution. They became slaves themselves but later they were released and God gave them a wonderful new home. Unfortunately, it was already occupied but that was ok because God told his people to commit genocide and even threatened to punish them if they didn't kill everyone. Although it is little reported, a funny thing happened on their way to this promised land. His people got upset that all the decisions were being taken by Moses and his brother and they protested to the pair, who immediately passed the problem upstairs. God's answer was not to mediate the dispute, nor even to show his favouritism, instead he sent a plague to wipe out his chosen people which was, luckily, stopped by Aaron's use of incense with only a few thousand dead. So that's alright.

It was later decided, by followers of a prophet of these chosen people that when God finally ends his little experiment, the Chinese and millions of others will be damned to eternal torment because they didn't follow orders which they never received and because they ignored God's son, who they hadn't heard of. Later still, God sent an angel to dictate a completely new set of instructions to an illiterate man who remembered it all and told little bits of it to lots of people so they could write it down and it would all be collected and put into a book after he was dead. A book which said it was OK to kill people as long as it was done in his name, which prompted them to go to war with everyone they met. That might seem a bit harsh but they had been told very clearly that they existed only to be God's slaves and, after all, rules are rules.

Really?
I hope you will pardon me when I say that I find all this just a little too much to accept. In fact, whilst I have been a little sarcastic in my account, the whole thing is utterly preposterous. Unbelievable to any modern man with knowledge of the world and a limited understanding of the universe. I'm sorry if this upsets you.

The whole story of religion is ridiculous when viewed without the blinkers of faith.

The neuroscientist Sam Harris puts it well,

"Religion allows perfectly sane people to believe, by the billions, what only lunatics could believe on their own".

To emphasis his point he explained,

"If you wake up tomorrow and think that saying a few Latin words over your pancakes is going to turn them into the body of Elvis

What is particularly puzzling about the Catholic version of holy communion is the fact that, with the most cursory of checks, the cracker is clearly still just a cracker after blessing and the wine very evidently does not become blood. Believing that they truly become the body and the blood seems like cannibalism, so I think that's probably a good thing. And yet the Catholic church teaches that the wafer and the wine actually become the body and blood of their saviour, not representative of, but in reality.

If the ridiculous non-miracle of transubstantiation was the only religious doctrine that gave us difficulty, things would not be so bad, but there are many far worse and not only in the Catholic church.

The vast majority of people in the world today are atheistic about the vast majority of gods in which humans have believed. We no longer get drunk to honour Bacchus. We no longer burn our children to pacify Baal or Molok, or drive ourselves into a berserker rage to kill for Odin. But billions still believe in the God of Abraham, worshipped by Jews, Christians and Muslims alike. And that god demands a great many observances that even hard-line believers shy away from. Take, purely as an example, some of the laws set out in the Jewish Torah, which Christians call the Old Testament;

- Children who disrespect their parents should be stoned to death.
- Wearing different types of cloth at the same time will get you killed.
- Using two different animals yoked together to plough your field is punishable by death.
- It is death to work on the Sabbath.
- We already know that God has a big problem with homosexuality, but interestingly this is only

mentioned twice in the Bible, whereas not eating shellfish is mentioned eight times.
- And remember, slavery is fine.

But we don't need to worry because it's OK now, Christians tell us, because mankind has moved on and has a different understanding of what God demands of us. But where did this new knowledge come from if it's not in the holy books?

We look on the actions of fundamentalist Muslims in the present day with horror and we are rightfully wary of the rise of new fundamentalist Christians. Moderates accuse such zealots of misinterpreting the words of the holy books and perverting the message. But by what right do Jews, Christians and Muslims choose which bits of religious instruction to ignore? If violence exists in the Bible and the Quran, which it most certainly does, aren't the zealots equally as justified in following these examples and instructions as the moderates are to follow the more easily digested sections?

Bear in mind that to make any personal choice about which parts of your religion you are happy to practice and which you will ignore, is to decide that you know best. That you know better than the people who wrote the books for God. This might sound reasonable, after all they lived a long time ago when mankind knew far less about the world, but at the core of all the Abrahamic religions is a belief that their holy books come from God. In the case of the Bible, we don't know who the authors were but it is accepted by Christians and Jews that, at the very least, they were inspired and guided by God. Many, of course, believe that God controlled directly the writing of the books and they are therefore without error. Inexplicably, these people also make choices regarding which parts are clear, which need interpretation and which can safely be ignored. Who gave them permission to do that?

Muslims believe that Mohammed was commanded to write by

the angel Gabriel and that God's messenger dictated the Quran. It is therefore perfect and is the 'last testament'. And yet a great many, who otherwise consider themselves good Muslims, still select which parts of their holy book they will obey. They may deny this and claim errors in translation, but this is clearly not the case. Muslims have not always felt the need to be so obscure and, even for those of us who do not read Arabic, there are so many translations which clearly show both peaceful and loving words and calls for violence. A secular analysis of the Quran proposes that the more violent sections were written by Mohammed later than the peaceful parts, after he had gathered a power base and no longer needed to worry about how his words would be received by those in power. Orthodox Muslims deny this but are at a loss to explain the differences in the message without the pretence of mistranslation or incorrect interpretation.

Whatever we may wish to believe about authorship of the holy books of the three monotheistic faiths, we are presented with a situation where both the zealot and the moderate claim the other is wrong. From the outside we can see that, in fact, they are both right. They are correct when they accuse others of misinterpretation or perversion of their holy books but they cannot accept that they are doing precisely the same, from an opposite perspective.

So confusing are both the Bible and the Quran; so full of internal inconsistencies and contradictions, that it is simply impossible to be true to all of it. It is, of course, for this very reason that a practice has long existed in all three Abrahamic religions of exegesis, analysis and discussion on difficult points and the creation of commentaries to better explain what they truly mean and how to apply them.

The people who carry out these tasks become revered in their own right and their works become part of a canon of holy scripture. Jews have the Talmud and Muslims have the

Hadith. Christians have not created their own official body of work which is seen as an add-on to the New Testament, but much writing exists which is considered wise and essential in clarifying the holy book and presumably the intentions of God. But by what right and with what authority do these people carry out this task? If these men are so learned and so able to interpret and explain the holy books, should they not also be some of the most committed of their co-religionists? And if so, why do they not accept the original material as needing no further illumination?

There is another point to consider. If these books are dictated by God's messenger or the work of individuals 'guided' by God, why has the creator not been clearer? If God is omniscient and omnipresent, why is he so obscure? If he demands our complete obedience, on pain of death and eternal damnation, why has he allowed his message to be so contradictory and so open to interpretation and error? For something so important that to get it wrong results in death and torture in eternal fire, God is worryingly vague.

Let's summarise a few key points:

- We have a universe that is so vast and so deadly that our place in it is probably unimportant and is certainly precarious and yet it was supposedly created for us.
- Humans were seemingly created imperfect and yet we can be blamed for our mistakes. The late Christopher Hitchens termed in *"created sick, we are commanded to be well"*.
- Holy books, either inspired or dictated by God, are so full of contradictions and so open to misinterpretation that practically anything can be read into them and, as such, can be used to justify any position and, as we have seen so often, any barbarity.
- These books make it clear that God demands

our obedience, on pain of supreme unpleasantness, and yet God either deliberately filled them with all manner of conflicting instructions, or at least allowed such opposing commands to be included. And when humans do the wrong thing, by actually following God's own words, we are to be punished.

- All three monotheistic faiths are clear that they worship the same god. This god not only gave the adherents of these faiths differing instructions, she allows them to kill one another in the millions based on these different instructions.

- And to add to the previous point, these holy books are so confusing that God allows her followers to interpret them in a host of ways, which gives rise to countless variations of worship even within the same religion. She then stands back as these sects with minor differences persecute one another and even try to wipe each other out.

But God loves us.

Now I may be being over analytical, but none of this makes any sense to me. I cannot believe these incomprehensible ideas and I certainly cannot believe in a god who would do any of it or allow it to happen.

I am a non-believer because it is the only sensible option.

Belief in a loving deity may be comforting but that doesn't make it true. I may choose to believe that the Faeries in my garden protect me from evil, but it would be hard to make you believe it too, without evidence of their existence and their intentions.

Carl Sagan said,

"Extraordinary claims require extraordinary evidence".

I would suggest that the notion of an omniscient, omnipotent, omnipresent God, who loves us, but is happy to punish us with eternal fire for breaching rules, about which he is unclear, is the most extraordinary claim ever made. I eagerly await the evidence.

WHY WOULD I OBJECT
TO YOUR BELIEFS?

I have no problem with what any individual believes, providing their beliefs do not cause them to do harm. I respect the right of people to believe whatever they wish. However, belief in a God or gods is very different to believing that you are good looking, your football team is the best, or your Dad is the toughest. Personal faith is a strictly private matter but religion always impact upon others, often in terrible ways. This is where I have an issue.

What you will read next may make you uncomfortable.
Your deep and sincere belief that your god exists, does not make it true. No matter how convinced you may be of the truth of your personal revelation or how certain you are that your holy book is either divinely inspired, the actual word of God or dictated by an angel, there is no reason for anyone else to accept it.

This may sound unpleasant, even aggressive but it is merely the truth. Whether it be personal revelation, an inner feeling or the words in a book, everything related to religious belief is nothing more than an opinion. I fully understand that there is no doubt in your mind and that you claim to 'know' your god is real but in an objective reality you do not know, you merely believe.

The neuroscientist Sam Harris put it very well during a debate in front of a Christian audience. He told them that according to Islam, every one of them was doomed. They would all go to hell and burn for eternity because they had not accepted Allah and his prophet Mohammed. Then he asked them how much sleep they had lost worrying about that proposition. The answer, of course, is none at all. He concluded by saying that this is precisely how the rest of us feel about Christianity.
Another popular way of expressing it is by referring to a list of old gods such as Baal, Odin, Zeus and a thousand others. The professional sceptic, Michael Shermer, said that all Christians, Jews and Muslims are atheists when it comes to those gods, he just goes one god further.

Despite misleading claims to the contrary, there is no empirical evidence for the existence of God, or of gods. There is nothing that can be pointed to which proves, beyond doubt, that divine beings exist. All the billions of believers base their convictions on the same things and therefore their mass belief may be discounted as easily as we would the word of a single individual. Every personal revelation that has ever taken place has done so within the matrix of religion. There has never been a recorded instance of someone, with absolutely no knowledge of Christianity, suddenly believing in Jesus. Every holy book in existence differs not only from other holy books but from countless versions of the same book; something of which most believers are unaware. A great many of these differences are so slight as to seem insignificant but how can there be any differences at all in something that is held up as so holy it should be relied upon by the whole world? A few of the differences are so profound and stark that they bring into question both their authorship and their meaning.

With the exception of conversions, an individual's religion is set by their birth and their childhood and it is usually set for life. Being born to Christians in the United States will make you a Christian, being born to Muslims in Saudi Arabia will make you a Muslim, being born to Hindus in India will make you a Hindu. Religion has thus been called an accident of birth. From that point, a child is raised in a faith by parents, siblings and the community, sometimes in a very relaxed way but often in ways which are elitist and divisive. Children are taught that their way is the only right way and that everyone else is wrong. And yet that conviction has absolutely no basis in fact.

Religion is taught as fact and as such it is a lie. Young children are not allowed to form their own opinions. They are not taught that some people believe one thing while others believe another, with equal conviction, equal fervour and with equal justification. They may be allowed such freedom of thought later but by then a pattern has been set which a great many never question because it never occurs to them to do so. Their faith is an integral part of their culture and of themselves and to lose it would be traumatic. And yet none of it can accurately be said to be true.

I fully accept and respect your sincerity when you speak of your Christian God and you explain his personality, his instructions for mankind and how he wishes to be worshipped, just as I accept the sincerity of Muslims, Hindus, Jews and people of every other faith when they tell me their very different story. I understand that to you and to them, the reality of your God is as stark and clear as how I see a table, a car, or a tree. But there are two problems. Firstly, no-one can prove their god is real. Second, they cannot all be right. Of course, they *can* all be wrong.

It may sound harsh but what you profess as fact and as truth is nothing more than your opinion. You believe it to be true because you were raised to believe, or something happened to convince and convert you, but you possess no knowledge, no artefact, no evidence of any kind which proves your beliefs. There are many arguments for the existence of God, most of them facile and weak, a few of them well thought-out and complex, but every single one of them fails.

Every argument has been refuted and demonstrated to be invalid, countless times. Modern religious apologists write books or make videos, offer speeches and take part in debates and they offer their 'proof' but in every case their reasoning is either patently nonsense, like the Ark Creationist Museum of Ken Ham in Kentucky, or it is a clever, but ultimately doomed, re-wording of an old method, like the revision of the Kalam Cosmological Argument by William Lane Craig. These ideas have been analysed and tested for three hundred years, since the Enlightenment began. Further back, in 1663, Galileo was arrested and charged with heresy for daring to agree with the idea of Copernicus that the Earth revolves around the Sun. The church knew this could not be true because the Bible says so. There are no new arguments in support of God and all the old ones have been proven wrong and dismissed.

But, true or not, why would I object to your beliefs? Because religious belief does not remain personal, it spreads. It seeks influence, initially to protect itself and later to pressure others into believing. It seeks power for the same reasons and then it uses that power in terrible ways, secure in the belief that whatever it does is justified by its service to God. In the past, when Christianity held real power in Europe, the church behaved in the same bloody, violent and merciless way, as a warlord. It oppressed, it persecuted, it tortured and it committed murder and massacre. All the terrors we see Islamic fundamentalists committing today were done by Christians when the church of Rome had real power. It has been argued that such things are the aberrations of men and not God but that begs the question, why would God allow such things, in his name?

There are other reasons for objecting to religious belief:

- Genital mutilation of children. In the west we abhor the mutilation of young girls in the Middle East and Africa whilst accepting the same done to boys in our own back yard as normal.
- Exemption from paying taxes and, in many countries, an obligation for people to pay a church tax to allow the state to support the predominant religion.
- Christian groups in the USA seeking political influence and power, in spite of the national myth that the country was founded by people fleeing religious persecution.
- Christian groups exercising real political power in many parts of the USA, by demanding that creationism be taught in school, alongside and equal

to science and, far worse, that evolution be taught as an unsubstantiated idea or banned completely. This undermines the principals of education and gives rise to a reduction in overall standards.

- Some USA Christian groups supporting and encouraging right-wing Israelis to illegally settle on land belonging to Palestinians because they hope to hasten a conflict which will become Armageddon and thus usher in the Kingdom of God.
- Some Christian churches, in particular the Catholic church, joining in common cause with hard-line Muslim states in pressuring the United Nations to make blasphemy a breach of international law. This would obliterate free speech.
- The Catholic church being partially responsible for the devastation caused by HIV and AIDS in Africa, by teaching that although the disease is terrible, it is still a sin to use a condom.
- The sexual abuse of children by priests and other religious people that should be trustworthy.
- The deliberate policy and written instructions of the Catholic church not to cooperate with law enforcement and to remain silent in cases of sexual abuse, usually of children. Where priests have been shown to be guilty the church has removed them to a place of safety and given them new jobs.
- Thousands of years of religious violence and billions of deaths.
- Teaching children that the god of their particular community is real and everyone else is wrong.
- The interference of religion in people's private lives. Dictating who one can or cannot marry, who one may have sex with and how that act is to be performed.
- The religious condemnation of people of differing sexual inclination, leading to ridicule, persecution and even death.

- Religion allying with secular powers for mutual gain. The crusades in which armies carried crosses blessed by the Pope as they massacred European Jews on their way to fight for the holy land. The church in the conquest of South and Central America and a policy towards the native populations of conversion or death. The first treaty signed by Nazi Germany was with the Vatican and all members of the clergy were instructed to remember Hitler in their prayers. Catholic priests in Rwanda in 1994, preaching that it was necessary for the Hutu to commit genocide against the Tutsi and the Twa peoples and even other Hutu of more moderate disposition.
- Bible stories that approve of slavery, torture, murder, rape and even genocide.
- The Quran, which carries very clear instructions to kill non-believers alongside passages about love and mutual respect.

I am aware that the above list is too long for easy reading but it could be much longer. Throughout human history religion has caused conflict and strife. There is a dark side to our nature. Without rule of law, we are far too eager to oppress one another. Religion not only taps into that urge; it justifies our darker deeds as actions in defence of a chosen deity.

If you wish to sit quietly at home and worship your cat as a god, I respect your right to do so. If your cat tells you to kill your neighbours, we will have a problem but apart from that, I'm fine with your choice. I might think you are deluded but it is not my concern. But the moment you begin to teach others to worship Tiddles and you speak on his behalf, you have founded a religion and trouble is just around the corner.

Whether you are a committed Christian, an observant Jew or a passionate Muslim, your views are both elitist and divisive. You may not feel that way but how can it be otherwise? You believe that your god, or at least your way of worship, is right and all others are, necessarily, wrong. You may not give much thought to others and you probably don't hate them but, in reality, it is absolutely necessary for their views to be wrong if yours are right. This is the underlying matrix in which moderate religious faith gives rise to fundamentalism and all acts of oppression, hatred and violence committed in the name of a god.

That is why, although I treat you with respect as an individual, I object to your beliefs and to all religious belief.

CHALLENGING RELIGIOUS BELIEF

(Originally An Article For An Atheist Magazine)

Greetings from the UK. It is November 2020 and like people all over the world, I'm in lockdown to protect myself from Covid 19, the new plague. But there is no rest for me. Your editor asked for an article with suggestions to help you to challenge the tactics and questions levelled by religious believers. What to say when they offer to save your soul, if only you would stop thinking and start obeying.

I am aware that many of you need no help from me and also that nothing you will read here is in any way new or even my own idea, it is merely a collection which I have acquired over the years and which I hope may be of some assistance. So, here goes.

I want to begin by making it clear that when challenging belief, it is important to do it respectfully and politely. No respect need be shown to the beliefs themselves, but we should always treat individual believers with kindness, unless they behave otherwise. And if they do become unpleasant, walk away. Do not match anger with anger, you will make no progress and it is a waste of your time and energy.

As non-believers, we consider ourselves free of superstition and able to employ clear critical thinking. We should therefore be aware that although it is an intellectual exercise for us, challenging a person's deeply held beliefs may threaten their whole world view and may be cause for genuine distress. This is an emotional issue and may drive them to react poorly but we have no such excuse and must hold ourselves to a higher standard. We must employ persuasion and facts and stay away from mockery and insults.

It is important to specify that, in what follows, I am mainly concerned with the three Abrahamic monotheistic religions, Judaism, Christianity and Islam. The Eastern religions tend to be either animist in nature or pluralistic (with multiple aspects of godhood), or closer to philosophy, like Buddhism. Either way, they are far less likely to cause harm as they are, usually, not as proscriptive as those I am focused on here. It seems that when belief revolves around a single god, with fixed rules decided upon by men, religion becomes more about power and control and can be shown to be a restriction on human progress and the cause of suffering and millions of deaths.

A small proviso must be added here with regard to the actions of some Hindus and some Buddhists. Religion always engenders strong emotion and we have recently seen sectarianism and violence from minorities in both faiths. However, this is almost exclusively political in nature and whilst the perpetrators may identify as one religion or another, their actions are not done in the name of their religion. An important distinction.

Try to reduce any confrontation. When two people argue, the only voice they each hear is their own. If your objective is to prove how smart you are, to demonstrate your superiority or to mock and insult someone, by all means be confrontational but be aware that your need to dominate is actually a weakness. If you genuinely seek to discuss religious belief and perhaps to try to change someone's mind, it is vital that, at the very least, they are listening. Do *you* listen to people who mistreat you?

Always begin by asking a believer to explain their position. This has two benefits. Firstly, it allows you to tailor your approach and not to be side-tracked into challenging something which they may not even believe. Secondly, it allows the other person to talk and to relax. Everyone's favourite subject is themselves.

Try to find some common ground. It may be the beliefs of others, or an individual's problem with something specific in their own religion but whatever it may be, it will create an atmosphere where both of you may contribute without simply butting heads. Once you have a rapport, introduce your ideas gently. You may be smart; you may be right but you will make no progress beating them over the head with your logic.

It is important for all of us to use reason, not blind faith. Here are a few examples to emphasise the point.

There are a number of documented cases where parents watched their child die from illness because they thought that resorting to medicine and not relying on prayer was an insult to God. Despite appearances to the contrary, these parents were not evil. They were otherwise good people who loved their child, but they sincerely believed their way was the only way. In other words, they simply had a bad idea of how the world works.

The Catholic church in Africa condemns the use of condoms, even though they have been proven to significantly reduce the risk of HIV infection and subsequent death from AIDS. The church does not want to see people suffer and die but it is convinced that its way is best.

In the USA, some states have bowed to pressure from evangelical Christians and include creationism in their school curriculum, alongside and sometimes instead of evolution. These people are not trying to reduce children's respect for science or to damage their futures, they genuinely believe their religious myths to be true and that evolution must therefore be false.

These three examples demonstrate why it is vital that we always use reason and not faith to manage our lives. We should always try to find the best answers and not be corrupted by bad ideas or be bound to living by rules created through belief without evidence.

Whilst I may not understand the finer detail of some scientific principles, I accept that the scientific process is valid. A scientist will formulate a hypothesis which makes certain predictions, then test that idea with experimentation and observation. Only if the observable results repeatedly match the predictions is the hypothesis considered valid. The whole process is then handed over to others to test and seek to disprove in peer review. It is a process focussed upon fact, not belief and discoveries must be supported by clear evidence.
Secondary to that is the practical application of technology

based on science. I do not need to know the details of the germ theory of disease or the principals of aerodynamics for me to trust medicine or to travel by plane. I am comfortable with the fact that the end results have been tested time and again to be consistent. My belief is not required.

Last but by no means least, scientific claims and discoveries are testable. Moreover, they are testable by anyone who is prepared to work hard enough to gain the correct qualifications and understanding.

Contrast the above with having faith in something that cannot be proven. Contrast it with following the word of another human being when they claim to understand what God wants.

Science seeks to expand human knowledge and it is required to provide evidence in support of its answers. Faith and religion claim certainty without evidence and often discourage further questioning or the seeking of knowledge.

"Trust in the Lord with all your heart and lean not on your own understanding". Proverbs 3.5.

This is seen as a good thing by Christians but a moment's thought shows it to be advocating the surrender of your mental faculties.

Two common statements made by believers;

"You should respect my beliefs".
Treating people with respect is a good thing but that is not the same as respecting their beliefs.

Firstly, why should I respect your beliefs? I don't have to respect your choice of football team or political party. Why is religious belief above criticism?

Treating believers as though they are not strong enough to face a challenge is not respect, it is condescending. Treating a religion as though it must not be questioned or criticised causes us to wonder what it is afraid of. Demanding respect for one's beliefs is to suggest they either will not withstand analysis or that those beliefs place the believer above the rest of us. The true purpose of this attitude is to excuse those making religious assertions from having to justify themselves.

"Atheists are just angry" (see also, *"atheists hate God"* and *"atheists believe the devil's lies"*, etc)
Even if this were true, it does not automatically make the religious story factual. Do not display anger and always challenge anyone who makes such a statement to respond to the message not the messenger.

In a challenging conversation about their faith, believers will sometimes try to move the goalposts. If you are countering their argument, or if they cannot refute your point, they will try to change the conversation by saying, *"well what about...?"*
Do not allow this. Keep them to the point. If their beliefs are valid, they should be able to answer you. Don't allow them to wriggle or you will spend all day switching from point to point and get nowhere. Simply respond with, *"OK, we can discuss that in a moment but first can we finish this point?"* Be strong but remember, always keep your iron fist in a velvet glove.

Answers to arguments
10 areas in which believers seek to prove their point with 'unanswerable questions'.

"Science can't explain ....."
The key word here is *can't*. What they are really saying is that science *hasn't* explained it yet.
There is nothing wrong with saying, I don't know. It is the beginning of enquiry. To say, *"I can't prove it, I just know"*, is not an answer, it is to pretend a certainty that you simply don't have.

The argument from ignorance is to say, we don't know, we cannot know and that is where God lies. That doesn't prove God, it only proves ignorance.

The argument is self-defeating because each time science answers a question about the universe, we push God further away. She used to live above the clouds, but where is she now?

Try this one. *"Scientific ignorance does not automatically grant your knowledge. For example, scientists don't know what came before the Big Bang and neither do you. If you can assert that is where God lives, without any evidence, I can assert that the universe itself is eternal and needs no creator. You will then demand that I prove my assertion but the point is, neither of us actually knows"*.

"You can't prove God doesn't exist"

True. I can't prove Smurfs don't exist either but do either of us believe in Smurfs?

Try dropping the following into the conversation:

"You're a thief. You steal things from others. Stop doing it".

The conversation will then go something like this;

"I'm not a thief".

"Prove it".

"I can't but there is no proof that I am a thief".

"That's right. You can't prove a negative but that doesn't make the opposite true".

The burden of proof lies with one who makes a positive statement. Not with one who refuses to believe it. Therefore, if the statement is that God exists, there should be sufficient undeniable evidence to support the assertion.

"Read the Bible. It's all there".

This is a common response but it often fails when questioned. Try coming up with an issue or problem and ask what the Bible actually says about it. Most people will not be able to answer. It is also helpful to be able to quote a few things from the Bible that are plain silly or which go against what we know of the world.

Surveys, carried out by Christian groups, have shown that only around 10% of Christians have read the Bible in full but 74% of Christians believe that the Bible has all the answers. In other words, the majority of Christians believe in what they *think* is in the Bible or what they are *told* is in there, but they have never cared to check. Incredibly, they have never bothered to actually check on something which governs their whole lives.

Most Christians live their lives by principals and rules given to them by other men and because this is begun when they are children, they never question it.

"Science is compatible with the Bible".

If we are to believe in the Bible in the modern world, it must be compatible with our modern knowledge. Many believers have been told that it is and have not checked. Newsflash; it's not.

Do we think that biologists have nothing to say about someone rising from the dead? Or that physicists are ok with someone walking on water. Or that Chemists won't challenge the idea that a person could be turned into salt? Or that a global flood, which left no evidence, is not a concern for geologists, or indeed for historians (we have masses of records left by the Egyptians, who had a thriving economy at the time but who seemingly survived the flood and failed to mention it).

No. The Bible is in no way compatible with science and our modern knowledge of the world and the universe around us. The same is true of the Quran. Muslims like to assert that the Quran contains many things that could not have been known at the time but each of the passages requires interpretation. Nowhere does the Quran contain clear statements about the natural world or about the future that do not require finding a meaning that is not specified in the text.

"There are religious scientists".

Yes, but where do they publish their ideas? In scientific journals for peer review, or in popular books for you to read? Which audience do they write for? Do they try to convince other scientists of their beliefs and rigorously defend their position in rational argument and with evidence in peer review, or do they seek to separate their beliefs from their science in some kind of split personality dualism? Or, worse still, make profound sounding statements to lay readers that other scientists would never accept?

"If there is no God, how did life begin?"
There are excellent theories which seem to be feasible, but in truth we don't truly know, yet.
But even if we never find out, why does my ignorance equate to your knowledge? I might be wrong but that doesn't automatically make you right. It only means that there is more work to do.
If I want to know the answer to this question, I go to a biologist or a chemist, who have studied and learned and have demonstrable knowledge of the subject. I do not go to someone with no training, who simply believes they are right, because they *feel* it or because they prefer to rely on an old book; like a priest or an apologist.

"You defer to experts, which is just like faith".
No, it isn't. We all defer to experts every day. Each time we eat a cheeseburger we accept that someone has proven it is not harmful (ok, bad example). Each time we get on a plane or in a car or use our phone we defer to others who have proven the technology works and that it works *consistently*.
All religious believers accept that science works, every day. Until they get to something that directly conflicts with their religion, like the evolution -v- creationism debate and then they quickly change their position.
Do we really believe that for centuries scientists have done amazing things to improve our quality of life, only so that now they can all lie to us about evolution? Do we truly believe that ridiculous conspiracy theory or do we believe that thousands of scientists all over the world, working on the problem for the last 150 years have all made a mistake?

Science is repeatable and testable. If we care to put the work in, we are all able to learn about science and technology, to test it and prove it for ourselves. The same is not true for the assertions of religion.

"The universe looks designed".

No, it doesn't. This is one of those pretend scientific statements that is foisted upon the public but which scientists would never allow to go unchallenged.

The universe is unimaginably vast and almost all of it is deadly to humans. The very atoms we are made of were formed in dying stars which were, in turn made from sub-atomic particles that were made in the Big Bang. We would not be here without the process of 13 billion years of cosmic construction and destruction. If it is God's work, it is incredibly time consuming and wasteful.

Each snowflake is unique but we fully understand the physics behind how they are formed and a god of snowflakes is unnecessary.

Water is chaotic. It takes continual heat energy to maintain liquid water. If you remove the energy, you get ice. That is order from chaos without the hand of a god.

Stars are formed from chaotic clouds of hydrogen. If there is enough hydrogen, gravity pulls it closer and tighter together until there is enough energy to ignite a new star, which 'burns' by the transition of hydrogen into helium. We understand precisely how this works, using the laws of physics.

There are a great many examples in all living beings which demonstrate flaws. If we were designed by God, she did a poor job.

If the universe was designed by God, who was it designed for? Certainly not us. As a brief aside, let's have a look at what was, supposedly, created with us in mind.

The edge of the observable universe is 46.508 light years from earth in every direction. That means it would take a very long time to reach the limit of what we can see from earth. And that is only if we could travel at the speed of light, which is

670,616,629 mph. In reality we could never reach the edge because the universe is expanding with increasing speed and we could never catch up. And that is the observable universe; we have no idea how much farther it goes.

How many planets are there? Well, this has to be an estimate. There are between 200 billion and 2 trillion galaxies in the observable universe. Our own galaxy, the Milky Way, contains between 100 and 400 billion stars and at least 100 billion planets and we have no reason to believe that the other galaxies are any different. (The exact number is difficult to estimate because low density stars are hard to detect at more than 300 light years away).
Take the lower figure in each case and multiply 100 billion stars in the Milky Way by 200 billion galaxies and you need a supercomputer to give an answer. And on average, so far, we have seen at least one planet for every star.

Our observations and the extrapolation from them, demonstrate that a star explodes and goes out every second and has done so since the beginning of the universe. All the heavy elements and indeed the building blocks of all life on earth, and perhaps elsewhere, have come from this process. Life, and mankind itself would not be possible without it.

All these figures are impossible for our minds to really take on board but the image is clear. The universe is vast beyond the ability of our language and our minds to comprehend. If God made the universe for us, why make it so vast? Why make it so dangerous and so violent?

Coming back to earth, we know, from the fossil records, that 98% of all living species on earth have gone extinct. Why was this necessary and what kind of god would design something so wasteful, so destructive, so violently terrible?

"The laws of physics might be the hand of God, you don't know".
This is just going back to the argument from ignorance. I don't

know, therefore God.

But even if we admit, for the sake of argument, a deistic god who created the universe and stepped back, that is very different from the theistic and incredibly self-centred view that God gets involved and did it all for us.

There was a time when we understood nothing and we used gods as the agents for everything. But slowly, we have come to investigate the unknown and every single time we investigate, we have come up with a scientific explanation. There has never been an instance where we discovered God. Not one. If two boxers fought twenty times and the same boxer won every time, who would you bet on for the next fight? There are a great many instances where a religious explanation has been replaced by a scientific one, like lightening and earthquakes. There has never been a single instance where a religious explanation replaced the scientific one.

"Reason is impossible without God because matter cannot think".
Look at a random collection of computer parts. On their own they cannot function. Assemble them and they perform logically and make choices and decisions.
"Aha! But the parts were designed and assembled!"
True. But computer parts are not made of self-replicating molecules. We are. Self-replicating molecules, subject to reproduction, mutation and natural selection, give rise to increasing levels of complexity and *improved functionality over time*. This lies at the heart of evolution which, despite what some people have been led to believe, has been demonstrated as reliable in many ways, over and over again.
And to return to the beginnings of life briefly, there are non-living self-replicating crystals in nature, so it is not improbable that the transition from chemical to biological occurred within that matrix.

Paley's watchmaker theory suggests that an uneducated man finding a watch on a beach would naturally assume there to be a watchmaker. But it is all about context. If that man believes that God created the sand and the ocean and the air, then yes, he will assume a watchmaker. But in reality, we live surrounded by watches. The sand, the ocean, the air, are all made of watches because we understand how they are formed. So, to automatically believe in a watchmaker as distinct from everything else is a fallacy.

I recently heard an answer to this assertion which made me smile,

"If you were walking along a beach and you found God, would you naturally assume there was an unknown god maker?"

"If reason is the product of unthinking matter, how can we trust it?" What other choice do we have? All thoughts and beliefs about God are created in the same way. How can we trust them?

"Reason isn't the only way to know the truth". Yes, it is. Even your beliefs about God come through reason. You may call it a feeling, or an inner presence but you understand those feelings through reasoning.

"My truth is different". No. Something religious apologists do often is try to re-define terms. Aron Ra, on his You Tube channel, clarified this issue by stating

"The truth is what the facts are" and *"If you can't show it, you don't know it".*

A fact is something that can be clearly and repeatedly demonstrated and is, consequently, accepted as true, without the need for belief. Truth is something which is in accordance with facts or reality. Religious truths are merely beliefs that do not withstand scrutiny. Adherents of one religion will claim a trait or personality for their god whilst another religion will claim something different for the same god. Both cannot be factual, therefore neither assertion may be relied upon to be true.

"The fulfilment of biblical prophecy proves the Bible and God".
Firstly, most prophecy is vague and can mean many things. If we look at a vague prophecy after something has happened which seems to fit, we are not seeing a fulfilment of the prophecy, we are making reality match the prophecy.
Why would God make vague prophecies? Why not be clear?
The Bible is also full of trivial prophecies which are almost guaranteed to come true because they are very likely. Prophesizing that the sun will rise, or a king will be born is not really hard to do and means nothing.
The gospel of Matthew admits that Jesus acted to fulfil a prophecy. How hard is it to fulfil prophecies that you already know? It proves nothing.

I am indebted to Paul Ens, a Canadian You Tube author under the name of Paulogia, who came up with the following checklist.

To be considered valid, a prophecy must be;
   • made clearly and demonstrably prior to the events predicted
   • intended to be a prediction
   • an extraordinary, non-mundane, claim
   • fulfilled by a single, clear, verifiable occurrence
   • not open to interpretation
   • not something people are actively working to fulfil

All biblical prophecies and those in the holy books of other religions, fail at least one of these tests and many fail repeatedly.

"The Bible is historically accurate".
No. It just isn't. Archaeology and other sciences have cast doubt on much of it. In fact, hopeful and religiously inspired archaeologists have worked in the region covered by the biblical narrative for nearly two hundred years, trying to find evidence of the stories but have found nothing which relates to events of the Bible. We should be grateful that the vast majority of them

were honest enough to admit their lack of success.

For example, we possess a vast array of documents and artefacts from ancient Egypt and we have even conducted DNA studies on human remains but there is absolutely nothing to show millions of Hebrew slaves ever lived there or that millions of people left all at once and spent 40 years wandering in a region smaller than Tasmania, or Andalucía in Spain, or the Republic of Ireland, or Lake Huron.

But even if it *was* accurate as history, it proves nothing regarding the existence of God.

Writing a semi-mythological history of a people is fine, but it does not mean the history is true and it does not mean we can add in other stuff, like creation myths and miracles and it automatically becomes true.

Which is more likely? That God decided to give her message to Abraham, an obscure nobody in an out-of-the-way backwater and expected him to father a people who would, eventually, spread the message to the whole world, rather than telling the Chinese, who already had a sophisticated written language and astronomy by the time of Abraham? Or, people made stuff up?

Even if, purely for the sake of argument, we accept the Old Testament as historically accurate, it does nothing to prove the existence of Jesus and even less to prove his divinity. The New Testament gospels differ from each other so much, and in significant ways on key issues, that they simply cannot be relied upon. Even church sponsored biblical scholars accept that they were written between 40 and 120 years after the crucifixion, by people who spoke a different language to the people in their stories and who lived in a different country from the events they portray and who were not themselves eyewitnesses. They are not history, they are demonstrations of faith by people already convinced of the divinity of Jesus.

The philosopher David Hume commented on the virgin birth,

"Which is more likely: That the whole natural order is suspended or that a Jewish minx should tell a lie?"

Lastly, we know that the creation myth in Genesis simply cannot be accurate. As an example, it has light and dark, day & night, existing before God created the sun and the moon. It is clearly written by people who had no knowledge of what was beyond the clouds. Even if the rest of the Old Testament is eventually proven to be at least an attempt to tell the story of a people, adding a mythological creation story to it does not make that myth true. And if we move forward to other events, like Noah's Ark and the tower of Babel, it becomes arrant nonsense.

"Everything that exists has a beginning. Everything with a beginning must have a cause. Therefore, the universe must have been caused/created by something that exists outside of space and time. That is God".
No. This is an assertion, not a logical truth.
Firstly, all we can truly say is that *something* must have existed before the Big Bang, but there is nothing to show that this was God.
Secondly, if the argument is that everything that exists must have been created, then we must admit, using the same logic, that God must have been created. By whom? The argument seems to rest upon a logical premise and then conveniently abandons its own logic when God is reached.

"I feel God within me".
"I know he is real and that he loves me".
"God speaks to me".
These are taken together because they all mean the same thing.

How do we know that such feelings are God? Mental illness would provide the same certainty, or it could simply be the interpretation of natural thoughts and feelings through a filter of existing belief. Despite much debate and even violence about the details, the concept of God is known worldwide. Therefore, no-one has ever woken up one morning, with no knowledge whatsoever of God and suddenly felt her inside. An individual may have had a feeling one day that they took to be the presence of God but they already knew of God and that affected the way they interpreted the feeling.

Feelings, however strong and however personally convincing, are not evidence.

Many Christians sincerely belief that God speaks to them and loves them and has definite ways in which he wants them to behave. But many Muslims are equally sincere in believing something totally different. Why would God choose to communicate in such a vague way, which allows peoples of very different faiths to believe that they are right and everyone else is wrong?

What about people of other faiths? There are millions of people today and billions throughout history, that have heard the voice of their god or gods, that have sought the truth about its nature and its mind, that have spent a lifetime in deeply sincere prayer and devotion. But they have not prayed to the God of Abraham, because they had never heard of her. If they are merely mistaken, God must be happy for them to be consigned to hell.

There are recorded cases of people killing others, even their own children, because they heard the voice of God telling them to. If we are content that such people are insane, why do we believe Abraham was sane?

It is clear that people can truly believe God speaks to them. But if someone believes God really spoke to them, why don't they believe people from other faiths who say the same? If their accounts of what God says are so radically different, how do we know who is hearing God and who is deluded?

"God answered my prayers".
What was prayed for? Was it something that absolutely could not have happened without God?

When people believe their prayers have been answered, they are really only saying that something happened that was improbable but not impossible and that they cannot explain it away. It does not mean that God is the only answer.

When you prayed for your grandmother to get well and she did, you gave thanks to God but did you give a thought to all the people whose prayers were not answered or to all the children dying needlessly before their fifth birthday? You think God was good for hearing and granting your prayers but if he did so at the expense of others, is he really good?

"My faith changed my life".
"I used to be a criminal/drug addict etc, but Jesus helped me to change".
I am genuinely happy for you. But belief doesn't need to be true for it to work.
The fact that you believed in something enough to feel helped and supported as you changed, is enough. It is also self-fulfilling. You believe you are being helped and you improve. You attribute the improvement to your god and it strengthens your belief and around and around it goes.

"How do you explain miracles?"
Christopher Hitchens paraphrased the philosopher David Hume by saying,
"What is more likely, that the laws of nature have been suspended, in your favour, or that you've made a mistake?"

We can discount the miracles of antiquity because they are either reported third hand or asserted by sources which are themselves questionable. There are contemporary accounts, from the time of Jesus, of other people performing miracles. Is the only reason we do not to believe in those accounts simply because they are not in the Bible? But we cannot use the Bible to prove the Bible so why discount all the other miracle workers that did not worship your god? So, either miracles are common and not the sole province of your god, or they are merely fabrications, believed because they seem to support your pre-existing beliefs.

It seems significant that the frequency of miracles drastically reduced as mankind progressed from accepting religious answers for everything, to a grasp of scientific understanding. Those miracles that do, very rarely, occur today are either explained away with investigation or they are reported second or third hand and not repeated upon further study.

Sathya Sai Baba was an Indian mystic who died in 2011. His followers believed that he regularly performed miracles like flying unaided and raising the dead and one million of them attended his funeral. Do Christians, Jews or Muslims believe these stories? If not, why not?

"Morality comes from God".
"You can't be moral without God".
"The Ten Commandments taught us how to behave".
First of all, if mankind had waited for the ten commandments to teach us not to behave like savages, our species would not have survived long enough to reach Mount Zion in the first place.
There are a great many cultures which have a moral code but who are not and have never been believers in the God of Abraham.

Morality is not a fixed idea. It differs from culture to culture and over time and although there are differences, all human cultures have morals. They exist to help us live together and are a necessary part of living in larger groups in a society with others. Even the morals we consider to be key, such as not stealing or not committing murder, are not shared by all humans. Some north American Indians believed that stealing from other tribes showed bravery. There are people in other parts of the world who used to eat their enemies, or shrink their heads as ornaments, in order to absorb their power.

It is simple logic that we all want to be happy and safe. To accomplish that we must have rules. No god is required to provide them, we just have to invent them for ourselves if we are to live in happiness and security side by side.

In Luke 14:26, Jesus says, "*If any man come to me and hate not his father and mother, and wife and children, and brethren and sisters, yea, and his own life also, he cannot be my disciple*". Where is the morality in this?

Another problem is the key tenet of Christianity. That of vicarious redemption. Jesus supposedly died for our sins. The idea that someone else can take responsibility for our crimes is utterly immoral. To pay a debt for someone may be a kind act, but to take on someone's sin is to absolve them from that sin. That cannot be said to be moral.

"*Without God, good and bad are arbitrary constructs with no real meaning*".

This extension to the moral argument is clearly nonsense. Does the holocaust cease to be bad when we deny the existence of God? Even the Nazi's, although convinced of their right to enact 'the final solution', knew that their actions had to be justified and could not be dismissed as mere whim.

If we accept that God is moral and is our example, we have to accept that ordering Abraham to kill his son as a test of faith was good and moral (a faith which God presumably already knew because he knows everything). We have to accept that ordering Joshua to commit genocide was good and moral, that killing people who work on Saturday is good and moral, and killing kids that disrespect their parents.

Not only is morality nothing to do with God, Christianity itself is not moral.

Here are three examples of Christian morality, according to the mainstream churches.

1. I am a good person; I give to charity and look after the old folk

in my street. I drink only in moderation; I never abuse people verbally or physically. I have never killed anyone. And I am an atheist. I will never be admitted into heaven.

2. Osama Bin Laden was responsible for the deaths of thousands and for his whole life he denied Christianity. But if, just before he died, he had accepted Jesus into his heart confessed his sins and renounced Islam, he would have been forgiven in the eyes of the Catholic church and would have been welcomed into heaven.

3. Sinners sent to hell will suffer *eternal* damnation. Regardless of the level or nature of their sins, they will suffer in the fire forever!

According to the tenth commandment, you can be punished for what you think, not just what you do.

Here are a few questions to highlight the problem:

- Would a good and moral God create an insect which lays its eggs in a child's eyes, for the larvae to eat their way out, causing suffering and blindness?
- Would a good and moral God create or allow natural disasters to claim the lives of millions?
- Would a good and moral God allow starvation and disease?
- Would a good and moral God allow war, in his name, where both sides believe in the same God but fight over minor differences of opinion as to how they should worship?

If you were in charge, would you do it differently? If the answer is no, people might think you are a monster. If you say yes, you admit the world is imperfect and that the God of Abraham wants it that way.

"God works in mysterious ways".
"God's ineffable plan".
"It is not given to us to know the mind of God".
"God cannot be judged by human standards".

These phrases are nothing more than excuses because religious scholars have no answers to the previous questions. They usually come up this when God has done something stupid or evil that needs to be justified. It should also be noted that preachers and religious apologists spend all of their time telling others precisely what God wants and intends and only fall back on this weak excuse when they run out of arguments.

"God makes people better".
By which scale do you measure that? What is your evidence?
The Nazi's believed in God. Millions have been killed in religious wars. It is true that atheists are just as able to kill but no-one was ever killed in the name of atheism.
Every prison has a chaplain or priest because prisons are full of religious believers who clearly don't believe quite enough to keep them from sin.

"What about love? You can't prove love but it exists".
This is neither a true comparison, nor is it accurate. Love is a product of the brain. It can be analysed in a lab to show the brain's activity, varying hormone levels and other physiological changes. Science can explain why we find someone attractive; why that person generates certain feelings in us; how these changes occur and how they have evolved.
Love is a brain state, just like belief. No-one would deny that belief exists but that doesn't mean God exists. God is outside of the brain and, if real, must exist whether we believe or not.

"We do bad things because God gave us free will. He wants us to choose him willingly, rather than being commanded to do so".
This sounds good, but we don't need every option available to us in order to exercise free will. If I have a few options, I am able to make a choice. If I am hungry, I can choose which wonderful food to eat. I don't need one of them to be poisonous to prove a point. God could allow us free will, to be able to choose him, without giving us the option to kill millions of other humans over a religious disagreement. If he is God and he loves us,

nothing is impossible, so why does free will have to include all the evil things?

The free will argument is only another way of saying, *"I have no idea why God would allow such things to exist"*.

If God is omniscient, he already knows precisely what we are going to say and do. If God cannot be surprised by us, how can we have free will?

"I know that there are other religions, but I know in my heart that mine is the right one".
How? Why is it more likely that your Christian religion is the right one? Billions of people believe in Allah. If you had been born in Saudi Arabia, you would believe in him too. Millions believe in Brahman, Vishnu and Shiva. If you had been born in India, you believe in them too. So, isn't a person's religion just an accident of birth?

But we don't need to look at Islam or Hinduism. There are so many different Christian faiths and they all think that theirs is the right way and everyone else is wrong. But why is one more likely to be more right than another? If we cannot answer that question with anything more than a personal feeling, why should we believe in any of them?

"Isn't it possible that we might find evidence for God?"
Is it possible? Yes. But nothing we have encountered so far makes it likely.

"If God appeared one day, would you change your mind?"
Possibly. But how would I know it was God and not a really advanced alien? If it was an alien who could time travel and whose science was so far beyond us that it seemed like magic or miracle, would we worship it, or is our idea of God more than that? If so, how would God prove himself to any of us?
If there was genuine unambiguous and undeniable evidence for a god, I would immediately accept that god. But short of that,

why would I choose to believe something so incredible without evidence?

There are other objections and reasons for not believing in God, but I think the above list will do for now. I hope it helps. Please remember that we must always respect individuals but we are not obliged to respect their beliefs.

The religious lobby continually strives to make challenging their world view a crime. In 2012 a group of Muslim nations, supported by the Vatican and some American Christian groups, brought a motion to the United Nations seeking to have blasphemy named as an international crime. This would have destroyed freedom of speech.
Freedom of speech is one of the most important human rights. It is important to exercise that freedom responsibly but it is vital that we use reason and critical thinking to live our lives and push back against those that would silence us and control our thinking in the name of their invisible friend.

Remember, at this difficult time, stay at home, stay safe, keep cheerful and exercise your mind.

ATHEISTS V AGNOSTICS

The Second Great Schism

Any student of religious history will know that in AD 1054, the Roman church officially separated from its eastern counterpart, after many years of conflict. Conflict which did not, of course, end there. Recently, there has been another great divide in religious thought, which is less well known.

With any form of human endeavour, when a movement becomes more popular and attracts more people, the initial orthodoxy is often overtaken by internal dispute. So it is with those who are not religious believers.

It may seem strange to those of us today who do not believe, to realise that the confidence to speak publicly about such matters is a comparatively recent phenomenon and is still limited in scope. Only one hundred years ago, anyone 'outing' themselves as a non-believer had to be cautious of offending others and of possible repercussions.   Indeed, the same is still true today in parts of the United States of America and in most Islamic countries. But for Europeans and those living in other, more secular, areas of the world, including those parts of the US not dominated by the Christian right, it has become a non-issue. Non-belief is perhaps something for personal reflection rather than shouting from a podium but it is a comfortable position to hold, nonetheless. However, a difference of opinion has arisen within these ranks.

Do you define yourself as an atheist or an agnostic?
This may seem a rather mild question but it can cause some dispute, even argument.

I am an atheist, although I rarely use the term; declining to be defined by a negative, I prefer to label myself a humanist. The finer points of identity aside, I do not spend my time proselytizing my lack of belief, but I will answer truthfully if the subject arises. When this occurs, there is often an exchange which goes something like this,

"Do you believe in God?"

"No, I'm an atheist".

"Ah, but you should say that you're an agnostic. Because you cannot know there is no God, the most you can honestly say is, 'I don't know'".

This divide between atheists and agnostics is becoming more common and it stems from a complete misunderstanding, which I hope to clarify here. Let's begin with a dictionary definition of each.

Atheist - A person who disbelieves, or lacks belief in, the existence of a theistic god. It is often, incorrectly, applied to non-belief in all gods

Agnostic - A person who asserts that nothing is known or can be known regarding the existence or nature of God or gods.

At first glance these seem remarkably similar but they are not. The first deals with belief, whereas the second deals with knowledge.

In practical terms, most atheists do not assert that there is no God. Rather, an atheist will say that he/she cannot belief in a god without satisfactory evidence. I should clarify at this point that atheists do not accept anything written in a book or any personal testimony as evidence but require something more substantial, which can be empirically tested to reliably give the same result. The difference between refusing to believe and stating that there is no God or gods may seem a fine distinction but it is an important one. Any positive claim carries a burden of proof. If we state that we do not believe, that burden rests with the person claiming that a God or gods exist. If, however, we are tempted into making our own positive claim that there is definitely no such thing, the burden of proof switches to us. And this is where agnosticism comes in.

To be agnostic, about anything, is simply to say that you do not know. This position does not rest on, or refer to, your beliefs. It applies only to what you actually know. It is therefore correct to say that everyone in the world is agnostic, in the religious sense, because nothing can be truly *known* about gods. Committed Christians, Muslims, Hindus and others will say that they 'know' but in reality, they are only affirming the depth of their belief. We need only consider that the various faiths make competing claims and therefore cannot all be right, to see that no human possesses empirically tested knowledge of the divine, however strongly and sincerely they might believe. When considering the Abrahamic religions, it is also fair to say that there can be no proof of an immaterial, invisible deity which exists outside our reality. We would first have to accept that the term 'outside our reality' had meaning. We might also point out that the Bible describes God in very physical terms in a number of passages.

So, perhaps non-believers would be more accurate to describe themselves as agnostic atheists? Admitting that they do not and cannot 'know' but not believing. This is technically correct but before we settle on the definition, we must look at something else. Probability.

Atheists, at least those that think deeply about their position, assert that their lack of belief is due to two things. The first is the simple truth that there is no evidence for the existence of gods. The second is that, in the modern world, with our ever-increasing knowledge of the universe and how everything works, the probability is that there is no God, or gods. Indeed, unlike previous generations who had little scientific endeavour on which to base their views, the modern atheist can state that the universe and what we know of its fundamental rules, functions perfectly well without the need to hypothesise about a creator or a guiding intelligence. We can also state, with confidence, that everything was not created in 6 days, beginning with the Earth and with the rest of the universe following a couple of days later.

In a humorous response to the complaint from believers that science doesn't know everything, the comedian Dara O'Briain, once said,

"Science knows that it doesn't know everything, or it would stop".

This is funny, at least in the way he delivers it, but it is also a good point. Only religion claims to have all the answers. Science is not a collection of answers, it is a process. But that process has given us some remarkable insights into the universe. Insights that the authors of the world's holy books and the greatest religious minds of history did not possess.

We know that the earth does not exist within a sphere of water, as the Bible describes it, nor is everything in the universe made from water, as the Quran affirms. We can also be reasonably sure that heaven is not above the clouds nor hell under the earth. We know there is no solid firmament, polished to shine like copper and with windows to let the water in as rain, over our heads nor does the Earth stand on pillars. We know that the sun and the moon are not merely lights placed in the sky to distinguish between day and night, a division which in Genesis already existed before God made the sun. We know that sun does not revolve around the earth. We should also acknowledge that, with the exception of the literalists who believe that the Bible is the inerrant word of God and therefore all scientific knowledge that does not agree with it must be wrong, most religious people also no longer believe these things. But all religions are based upon outdated ideas, such as these highlighted from the Bible and cherry picking is the only way such obvious fallacies can be reconciled with the modern world.

Every culture on earth has its own creation myth. Often involving gods or animals that died to create the earth or had parts lopped off by other gods, or something equally far-fetched. To our modern eyes they are clearly false and are seen as little more than amusing folk tales but Jews, Christians and Muslims cling to their own myths as if they are somehow different and therefore exempt from such critical thinking.

The biblical authors thought that God lived above the clouds. Later religious thinkers claimed that he existed within our universe but somehow unseen. Today it has become popular to claim that God created the universe and lives outside it. As human knowledge expands, God is driven further away. Those that accept the idea that everything must have a cause and that this proves God created the universe, must answer honestly a question: If, by your own logic, *everything* must have a cause, who caused God? It is intellectually dishonest to assert something as truth and then automatically exclude God, just because it suits.

For atheists then, the probability that God does not exist weighs upon the agnostic position. It is impossible to prove a negative and whilst it is true to say that such knowledge is therefore impossible, it is nonetheless a valid position to say it is likely that all gods were invented by men and that the monotheistic God is simply a development from the older pantheons and is, therefore, no more believable.

The late Carl Sagan said,
“Extraordinary claims require extraordinary evidence”.

The late Christopher Hitchens repeated the phrase and added *“That which is asserted without evidence, may be dismissed without evidence”*.

If we consider how much more we know than it was possible for our ancient ancestors to know, we see that the claim a creator God exists and, moreover, that he loves us and cares what happens to us, is far more extraordinary than any scientific idea. Because the religions of the world make positive claims about the existence of a God or gods, the burden of proof rests with them.

The Abrahamic religions were founded between 4000 and 1400 years ago, in a time when men knew little of our own world and absolutely nothing of what existed above the clouds. Without better sources of information, it was perfectly reasonable to accept the religious worldview. But as human knowledge increases exponentially, the religious position remains unchanged, unproven and untenable. Slowly but insistently, scientific explanations for the world's mysteries have replaced religious ones but the reverse has never occurred.

To be agnostic is valid and applies to most of us when we think about most things, but atheists have every right to refuse to 'believe' in a God without evidence.

I freely admit that I do not 'know' there is no God. But if the question were to be outlined on a scale of one to ten, with one being absolute proof of God's existence and ten being absolute proof that she is fictional, the honest agnostic position would not be a comfortable five, halfway between the poles. It would be eight for most people claiming to be agnostic and nine point five for some of us.

Put this scenario to the next person who claims that agnosticism is the only honest position. Explain the way human knowledge has consistently pushed God further away and made belief in religious creation myths impossible, then ask them about their own position on the scale. The result may surprise them.

ATHEIST OR ANTI-THEIST?

I have written a number of blogs and articles on religion and I thought it time I came clean about my personal position, in detail. That I do not believe in a God or gods is apparent but there is more. I usually strive not to be too strident or vehement in my assessment of God and religion but this time I will be brutally honest.

Let me begin with a definition and an explanation.

Despite countless attempts by religious apologists to assert otherwise, atheism is neither a religion nor a world view. It is simply the absence of a belief in any god. Atheists come in varying degrees of certainty but at the core rests a refusal, or perhaps an inability, to believe in supernatural creators and overlords without sufficient evidence. And it should be pointed out that, regardless of sophistry and clever argument, absolutely no evidence exists. It should go without saying that arguments are not evidence.

From being a casual Christian, due to childhood education, in my teens I discovered a Jewish heritage and, perhaps in a search for an identity, I became an ardent Jew. Some years later, for reasons that had nothing to do with any personal trauma, but rather a gradual awakening through reading and learning, I became an atheist. You may have read a more in-depth account of that journey in the introduction to this book but suffice it to say that at the end I was as vehement in my condemnation of religion as I had been in support of Judaism. But that was not actually the end.

Through the passing years and with what passed in my mind as maturity, I eased away from a desire to prove every believer was deluded and religion was an evil mechanism of social control. I never changed from that assessment of religion but I did become more mellow and a little more respectful of individuals, if not their beliefs. I also came to understand that using the label atheist was to describe myself with a negative. Whilst it was true that I did not believe in gods, neither did I believe in faeries, unicorns or superheroes. There is no word for these non-beliefs and saying I am an atheist is equally unnecessary and tells people nothing about me.

I am a humanist. Not believing in gods, I accept that I must take personal responsibility. I must take the blame for things I do wrong and take credit for things I do well. I must join fellow Humanists in caring for people, animals and the planet and I do not have the comfort, or the excuse, of supernatural interference.

All of the above being true, I have not lost my conviction that the existence of gods is, at the very least, extremely unlikely. It is usually said that there can be no proof that God does not exist, but there are some very clever arguments to demonstrate that the existence of the Abrahamic God is logically impossible. Here is one that relates to the claim of omnipotence. You may be familiar with it; it is certainly not my own.

Can God make a stone so heavy that he cannot move it?
If he cannot make absolutely anything, he is not omnipotent.
If he makes the stone and then cannot move it, he is not omnipotent.
Therefore, the idea of an omnipotent god must be false.

This is clever and convincing but, for now, I will simply stick to the accepted position that there is no reason to believe in a God without evidence. But what do we mean by God?

Other than a loss of popularity, there is no real difference between believing in the single Abrahamic God of the Jews, Christians and Muslims and the old pantheons of the Romans, Greeks and others. In fact, because the old gods were clearly just 'man writ large', I would suggest that they are more credible, in that they do not struggle under the burden of being perfect and are easier to explain. But there is little point in arguing against the existence of a Zeus or an Odin, largely consigned to obscurity except for history and fantasy. The later monotheistic god, be it called Yahweh, God or Allah, is a very different matter. In analysing and defining this deity we can only refer to the religions and their supporting holy books for our knowledge. And what we find is deeply unpleasant.

In the most effective and long running public relations campaign of all time, the three religions have tried to convince mankind that their God is omniscient, omnipresent, omnipotent and, the claim that is hardest to justify, that he loves us. A critical study of the holy books, not to mention the horrors committed by God and in God's name, demonstrates this to be a lie. There are far too many examples to list, but here are a handful:

Allowing other tribes to populate the promised land and then commanding his followers to commit genocide.
Condoning slavery and even providing rules for how it should be run.
Wiping out all life on earth because of a grievance with humans.
Being party to the torment and torture of an individual, poor old Job, in order to win a bet with Satan.
Causing and/or failing to prevent natural disasters and disease that have claimed billions of lives.
Being so unclear about what he wants that men have destroyed each other for centuries in disagreements over her intent.
Revealing herself and her desires in such a limited way that the majority of mankind were unaware of her and then decreeing that anyone who doesn't love her, or who doesn't obey her laws, should be killed.
Allowing her son to introduce the vile idea of damnation and eternal torture.

"Religion is a totalitarian belief. It is the wish to be a slave. It is the desire that there be an unalterable, unchallengeable, tyrannical authority who can convict you of thought crime while you are asleep,

The late great Hitch was a master at combining erudition with vehemence, but I think his description is accurate.

If we are speaking of the God of the three Abrahamic religions, she seems too cruel, too capricious and too uncaring to ever be worthy of worship. Consider; we are created with flaws, then punished for them. Given free will, we are punished if we exercise it in a way God dislikes. Commanded to love a God who clearly doesn't give a damn for us, we are condemned to eternal torture if we don't love, worship and obey.

When asked what he would say to God if, when he dies, he found he had been wrong, Stephen Fry said he would ask,
"Bone cancer in children, what's that about?"

Stephen Fry is a decent and gentle soul. I would not be so polite.

There is a reason why so much killing and horror has been enacted in the name of God and religion and it is not, as apologists would have us believe, down to human failings or free will. It is because there is so much justification for it in the Bible's terrible legends and because the Quran, written partly as an instruction manual, actually commands it.
The reason that Jews, Christians and Muslims do not all behave as barbarians is that the vast majority are decent people, despite not because of their faith and as such they cherry pick what they will adhere to and carefully ignore the more outrageous

passages such as killing disrespectful children or killing the infidel wherever you may find him. Indeed, in the modern world we may take some solace in the truth that so much of what is found in these 'holy' books is so patently false, or so sickeningly disgusting that most people cannot believe it.

We abhor Islamic fundamentalists who are prepared to kill for Allah. We see them as violent fanatics and we are told that they are not 'true' Muslims. But this is a deliberate falsehood, specifically designed to hide the truth. When these individuals commit their acts of terror, undertake an honour killing or oppress non-Muslims, they are not misinterpreting their holy scripture, they are simply being completely true its words. But before Christians, or anyone raised in a nominally Christian country, are tempted to feel a sense of moral superiority, we must consider that Islam is 600 years younger than Christianity. We must look back over the history of Christianity and keep our eyes and our minds open to the countless examples of genocide, persecution, oppression and casual violence committed in the name of Jesus meek and mild.

We should also admit two things. That were it not for Martin Luther, the Catholic church would probably still be more intent on abusing the gullibility of believers, in order to amass wealth and power, than in matters spiritual. And that, were it not for the Enlightenment, Europe and the Americas would still be under the oppressive heel of a church comfortable with any form of atrocity in support of spreading the faith and maintaining power.

"My concern with religion is that it allows us by the millions to believe what only lunatics or idiots could believe on their own".
Sam Harris

With respect to Sam Harris', I would say that in addition to belief, religion urges us, by the millions, to judge our fellow man, harbour ugly and violent thoughts and to commit crimes against humanity that only a psychopath would do alone. When a holy book fails to condemn slavery, makes women into an underclass and promotes violence as a solution and is still viewed as either the inerrant or the inspired word of God, we can hardly be surprised at any horror committed in the name of that god, no matter how vile.

It is for this reason that, although I now prefer to call myself a humanist, I remain atheistic. More than that, I am happy that such a being is unlikely to exist because I see the monotheistic God of the three Abrahamic faiths as evil.

In the opening paragraph of his book The God Delusion, Richard Dawkins wrote,

"The God of the Old Testament is arguably the most unpleasant character in all fiction: jealous and proud of it; a petty, unjust, unforgiving, control-freak; a vindictive, bloodthirsty ethnic cleanser; a misogynistic homophobic, racist, infanticidal, genocidal, filicidal, pestilential, megalomaniacal, sado-masochistic, capriciously malevolent bully."

This caused controversy at the time and still does but it is entirely accurate. But I would go even further.
There is nothing in the New Testament to change Professor Dawkins' view. The new version of God may be presented as loving, but that obscures things like the introduction of eternal torture in hell, Jesus' injunction to hate and abandon your family to follow him, to give no thought to tomorrow and the idea that not only is he the only route to salvation but that not loving him carries a harsh penalty. What would we call someone who threatened us with harm whilst commanding us to love them or else? The term psychopath comes to mind again.

On the other hand, Islam was given to the world some six hundred years after Jesus and in the Quran, the idea of an all-loving God is replaced with a deity much more like that of the Old Testament. Oppressively authoritarian and demanding that his followers be slaves, utterly subservient and happy about it, Allah commands that Muslims lie and kill and do anything in order to ensure he is obeyed, to point of forcible conversion or enslavement of the whole world.

Muslims like to claim that Islam has never been forced onto anyone and indeed, the Quran does make the point that there is no compulsion in religion but what else can we call it when a group of people are inspired by their new faith to attack and conquer their neighbours and then repeat the same behaviour further afield for hundreds of years and when conquered people are given a choice of conversion, slavery or living as an underclass, paying a tax specifically for non-believers?

Christians and Jews, quite rightly, scoff at claims that Islam is a religion of peace but they refuse to acknowledge the truth of their own history and continue the promotion of dogma at the expense of human dignity and well-being. It should also be mentioned that the great campaigner against church corruption, Martin Luther, was a vehement and deeply unpleasant anti-Semite. Apologists of all three faiths would have us believe that we are better off with God and that, as mysterious as it may be, God has a plan for our benefit. I think the facts suggest the opposite.

I am appalled at the ridiculous claim that an omniscient, omnipotent, omni-present God actually loves us and that all the horror in the world could be stopped by him, except that he has a plan for our benefit that we are not allowed to know. I think Hitchens had it right, that to believe in this is to choose slavery.

In conclusion. I am not only an atheist; I am an anti-theist. Even if it were proven that God existed, I would refuse to bow down to such a malevolent creature.

A QUESTION TO BELIEVERS

My question is a simple one and for a great many people I am sure the answer will be equally straightforward. At least it will initially seem so. As we delve deeper, however, I hope to demonstrate that the answer to my question is exceedingly complex. My question is this,

Why do you believe in God?

I should say at the outset that, whilst I understand this topic to be fraught with risk, it is not my intention to insult or upset anyone. I am aware that, for some, it has become all too common to cry the words *"I'm offended"* at anyone who speaks contrary to their personal beliefs and that these people expect by doing so, that some form of censorship, if not punishment, will be administered. Unfortunately, for such people, I utterly reject the idea that religious belief should be excluded from question or challenge.

It is the assertion of many 'people of faith' that everyone should respect their beliefs and that any criticism is automatically ill mannered or even blasphemous. I firmly believe this to be a contravention of the valuable right of free speech and a slippery slope which leads towards too much power in the hands of special interest groups, who need only to cry foul to have their will imposed. As I write this, a number of Muslim states, supported by the Vatican and hard-line Christian groups in the USA are actively petitioning the United Nations to pressure all member countries into making blasphemy a criminal offence. Once such a law is passed, freedom of speech is impossible.

Nonetheless, whilst remaining a staunch advocate of personal freedoms, I am not a heartless iconoclast and I do not make a habit of deliberately upsetting others. If what you read here angers you, I would suggest the problem lies with your own world view. If it simply upsets you, I apologise.

My question is directed towards followers of the three main Abrahamic faiths, Judaism, Christianity and Islam. I place them in the order of their creation and no preference or ranking is implied. These three, whilst seeming so contrary to each other, often violently so, are all related and are ultimately based upon the creation story, mythologised history and religious teaching of the Hebrews; later to become the Jewish people.

The Christians retained the old Jewish texts but they focus on the New Testament. Their religion, founded by St Paul, is centred around the story that the son of God came to earth. St Paul and the church are seemingly happy to ignore Christ's own words, that his role was not to change the old rules but to fulfil them and that he was sent to the Jews alone.

Islam too, whilst being based upon revelation and recitation to the Prophet Mohammed by the angel Gabriel, contains, at its core, much of the Jewish Torah and is clearly a development from what Christians call the Old Testament. Indeed, Muslims call their Quran the Last Testament and freely acknowledge the link to their two sister faiths.

This three-way familial association makes it all the more tragic that adherents have spent many hundreds of years trying to kill each other and begs the question why God would allow such misunderstanding of his wishes and such horror, committed in his name. But that is straying off the point.

We may safely begin by addressing my question to Jews, Christians and Muslims equally. In this modern age, so full of understanding and of evidence-based wonders derived by scientific enquiry and put to use by technology forged purely through human innovation, why do so many people still profess a belief in God?

The vast majority of Christians asked this question will respond that they know in their hearts that God exists and that he loves them. They are secure in the comfort of personal conviction. Jewish people appear, at first, somewhat more practical and would certainly never claim that God loves them unconditionally. Their history aptly demonstrates this not to be true. But they are still convinced of God's existence and that he has a plan for them. The Muslim position, as may be expected, is a development from the Jewish stance, but with the Christian unquestioning adoration of God as a significant influence. They are also convinced of God's plan but they believe that Allah turned his back on Jews and Christians and gave Mohammed very strict rules, which they must follow whilst still on earth because all men are born to be slaves to God.

Regardless of which particular religion is considered, the true believer will claim a personal relationship with their maker and, whilst using the holy books to guide their lives and the way they worship, they will anchor their faith in that very individual and internal feeling.

Let us be clear that there can be no proof that God does not exist. The best that atheists or rationalists may do is to state that there is no evidence for God's existence. They may go a step further and refer to scientific advancements that indicate the universe can be explained without recourse to God. But in the face of personal faith, based upon the certainty of inner feelings, all such rational argument is ineffective. So, if we cannot use critical thinking to argue against personal faith, we need to understand how believers arrive at their strong conviction.

The accepted path to personal faith is divine revelation. For a few, this actually means a personal encounter with God, or an angel or a miraculous event, but for the majority it is merely a feeling that grows over time, fed by the words of preachers and the holy book to become all-encompassing and utterly commanding. They attribute this to God putting faith in their hearts. There may be moments of weakness and doubt, but in the main they remain steadfast to what they know to be true. The problem with this explanation, whether it is the cataclysmic conversion of St Paul on the road to Damascus or the slow realisation of someone in 21st century London, is that this process does not exist in a vacuum.

Whether arrived at by direct revelation or by a growing of the holy spirit within, all those that profess this wonder of faith do so within a culture and a history that supports them. In other words, they already know about God. It has been said that no matter how firmly you believe, your religion is based upon an accident of birth. Born in the west, to Christian or Jewish parents you will probably follow their path. Born in other parts of the world or to Muslim parents you will, almost certainly, be Muslim. Even those that convert later in life do so through an acquired knowledge of their chosen faith. Their decision may seem to them to be unavoidable and not made through logical choice, but without knowledge of the new way such a change would not have been possible. There have been no instances of a Christian waking up one day as a Muslim, never having heard of Islam, nor vice versa.

It is clear then, that all religious belief, whether arrived at by the education and indoctrination of the young or by a direct personal feeling, must be rooted in the traditions and rules which underlie our culture. It is also clear that, ultimately, these influences are centred upon the holy books.
Even if you claim divine revelation you are constrained by your prior knowledge of your religion or of the alternative religion you prefer. The only possible exception to this that could be admitted would be the founding of a completely new faith, with no elements of those already in play. That is something mankind has never seen. Even Judaism reflects many values found in other, earlier faiths. Going back to the dawn of civilisation, every religion in the world, no matter how different from others, has been either a development of something already existing or a synthesis of two or more. Even the convicted con artist Joseph Smith when founding Mormonism, supposedly by divine revelation, could not disguise that fact that the angel Moroni, in dictating to him, spoke in the language of the King James Bible, translated from the original Hebrew,

Aramaic and Greek two hundred years before but seemingly, for reasons unknown, preferred by angels.

There is only one religion I can think of which might qualify as unique and that is Scientology. This strange phenomenon, more cult than religion, was invented by the science fiction writer, Ron L Hubbard. He had previously said in an interview that whilst writing was fine, the best way to make money was to invent a religion. He went on to do just that and yet there are still many who believe it and pay fortunes to the organisation he left behind. The existence of the Mormons and the Scientologists is clear evidence that people can fool themselves into believing almost anything.

But if our conscious or unconscious decision about which religion to follow, is based upon our knowledge of the holy books and the traditions and culture they have inspired, how can we be certain that the books themselves are true?

In order to justify the religious argument at this point there is an amount of circular logic employed. I believe in what the book tells me -- I know the book to be true because of my personal faith -- My faith is based upon the book. Whilst believers are utterly and honestly convinced of what they say, there remains a gap in the logic.

Once we accept the inescapable logic that faith cannot exist without prior knowledge of its source and that such knowledge has to be a part of a believers' culture or that of a nearby culture, we can only determine that such faith is ultimately based upon believing the words of a book. We then arrive at a discussion about the creation of the book and whether it can be trusted to portray an accurate picture.

There exists a vast body of information on the origins of the holy books of the Abrahamic religions and for at least two centuries scholars have applied various methods to better understand how and when they were written and by whom. However, for my purpose it is not necessary to delve into this field. It is sufficient to say that the holy books were written by men; that the men were inspired by their existing belief in their God and that this belief came from other material and verbal traditions, myths and legends. Of course, Mohammed is clear that the Quran was dictated to him by an angel and is thus the actual word of God and many Christians believe that their New Testament was, at the very least, put into the minds of the authors by God and can also be considered without error. In accepting these claims, we are returned to the circular logic above. Such a belief in the word is only arrived at by a belief in the concepts generated by the word and so on.

Leaving aside the origin of our opinions about God herself, it seems an unavoidable conclusion that all religious belief, whether through revelation or learning is founded upon one's own very personal feelings. But can we trust our feelings? Muslim fundamentalists 'know' that their reading of the Quran is the only correct one and they 'know' what Allah expects of them. Likewise, Christian fundamentalists 'know' that the Muslims are wrong and only *they* have the truth. But it goes deeper than a difference in interpretation or the words of different books.

How can we be certain that our mind is not playing us false? Individuals that are plainly delusional believe in their delusions without any room for doubt. A psychopath truly believes he understands the world and his place in it better than the doctors who treat him. I am not suggesting that religious people are delusional or mentally ill, but we all see the world differently and we are all convinced that what we see is more accurate, more 'true', than the perceptions of others. If we undergo a religious conversion, we are even more convinced that we had previously misunderstood and now all is revealed. No-one is more zealous than a convert.

If a man tells you that a tree in his garden is a manifestation of

God and it is telling him how to live, you may be forgiven for thinking that he needs help. But you cannot actually know he is mistaken. If you tell me that God is Allah or Yahweh, or that Jesus died and was resurrected, I may tell you that you are wrong but I cannot prove it. I cannot disprove God or your relationship with him. But I can question why you think such a thing. I can also effectively demonstrate that your thinking, as honest as it may be, is affected by a number of very understandable, easily explained, factors that have nothing to do with divine revelation but everything to do with tradition, culture and shared social values.

We can never know whether Abram was really addressed directly by God when he was commanded to change his name, travel to another land and be the father of a new chosen people. We can accept that the men who wrote down his story and the rest of the Jewish Talmud truly believed that they were doing God's will, but we cannot prove that was the case or whether they were simply influenced by and acting upon a mythology born over preceding centuries. The Christian and Muslim books too were presumably written by honest men, but we have to at least admit the possibility that they may have been honestly mistaken.

For religious people today I believe I have shown that their faith is a part of their education and is based upon tradition and culture, even if they feel a personal link with their deity. I have also shown that anything thought or felt by human beings can be either true or false and that, internally, we have no way of knowing which. Self-analysis is like using an incorrect rule to measure distance. If we cannot be absolutely certain the rule is accurate, we cannot trust the measurement it gives.

In conclusion I would suggest the following.
Whilst the existence of God cannot be disproved, it is illogical to base a complete belief structure, which dictates your whole life, upon thoughts or feelings that *may* be in error. Galileo was

a product of his time and to not believe in God was 'almost' unthinkable. Nevertheless, he said,

"I do not feel obliged to believe that the same God who has endowed us with sense, reason and intellect, has intended us to forgo their use".

He was appealing to the power of the church, which threatened to kill him if he continued to speak of his scientific understanding of the solar system, but I think it demonstrates another point. If God is a fiction, we can safely give up any such belief, but if she is real surely she cannot object to us using the faculties she gave us to manage our lives and our planet without recourse to her.

Believers speak of God giving us free will, but if we were given it only to test whether we would obey him, it seems a strange experiment. A being who is supposed to be omniscient and who must therefore be able to see the future would already know if we would pass the test and the test would be unnecessary. If she needed to test us because he cannot see the future, she is not God.

Theism is a belief in a God who is obsessed with the minutia of human lives whilst caring nothing for our suffering. She created us with faults and is happy to punish us for being true to our nature. Rather than reveal herself directly to all mankind, she made herself and her wishes known to only a handful of people and in a number of very different ways. Being omniscient, she must have known that doing so would cause us to seek each other's destruction, all in her name.

Deism, on the other hand, is the belief in a creator, a prime mover, that does not concern itself with us and therefore need not be worshipped. This is, in effect, indistinguishable from atheism in most ways and allows us to take responsibility for our own actions or inactions. Carl Sagan said that not believing in God is understanding that it falls to us to change the world.

In the early part of the twenty-first century, it seems a logical and even a sensible choice to be either a deist or an atheist. Technically, we can be both, as atheism is lacking a belief in a theistic God. As we can clearly see that belief in a personal God is subject to our own, possibly faulty, reasoning and that we cannot know whether we are in error, it must be right to abandon such beliefs in favour of something that we can rely upon without resting upon our own feelings.

If an omniscient God does exist, she would not only approve of our maturity, she would already know it was coming. If she is surprised or angered by our decision to think for ourselves, she cannot be God.

ANSWER TO A FUNDAMENTALIST'S THREATS OF HELL.

The following was first used when I received an ugly and vociferous response to a comment I posted on YouTube. My comment was on a video extolling the virtue of believing in Jesus Christ and warning viewers that to not do so would lead them to hell. My words were respectful and referred to the difference between fact and faith. I merely pointed out that whilst we might sincerely believe in God and Jesus, we cannot know. This prompted a tidal wave of disagreement, most of it passionate but not aggressive but one individual was incensed and raged at me. At one point he even told me he would delight in seeing my children burn. Of course, most people do not think in this ugly way but all religions have their fair share of those that really do.

Over the years, I have encountered a number of such vile people, always Christian or Muslim, never from other faiths, which may be significant or may simply reflect the direction of my own online activity.

I became tired of repeating myself and I now just copy and paste the following:

The Bible and the Quran and the traditions based on them are full of threats about what happens to non-believers and to people who turn away. Those threats are always terrible. Even the more moderate of religious believers seem keen for the rest of us to burn for eternity. For example, the Old Testament was pretty awful, filled with genocide and violence but at least our troubles were over once we died but with the coming of Jesus as saviour and his intercession with a supposedly loving god, we see reference to a hell and an eternity of suffering. Six hundred years later, we find Mohammed telling us it is God's will that non-believers are met with violence and apostates must be killed. But why?

Why would a loving god want to treat people that way? Why would an all-powerful, universe-creating super-being even care how humans behave? Why would an all-knowing god need every human on earth to worship him and to do it in very specific ways and, in the case of Islam, only in a specific language?

Human leaders cannot allow dissent because it threatens their position but what does your god have to fear? If it has already been decided that when the end comes some will be saved and others will perish, why not just leave folks alone? If your god really is omniscient, then he already knows what is in men's hearts and he already knows who will and who will not be there at the end. So what's the point?

By all means believe, that is your right. But unless you have the ability to discuss the specifics of your religion in a calm and rational manner; unless you can provide sound reasons and decent proof that you know something we don't, just leave the rest of us alone.

We are not interested in your ridiculous preaching and threats. We have no reason to believe in your god and so your threats of hell are also meaningless. But your delight at the prospect of the suffering of others does not make you a righteous person, it makes you a deeply unpleasant one. I wonder if your god would even want you.

Postscript

I have occasionally met such individuals on a face-to-face basis and I have found that remaining calm and smiling and answering them quietly with the same response is a sure-fire way of creating in them a form of religious apoplexy that is wondrous to behold. Is that cruel of me?

GOD OR GODS?

If you are an unbeliever and curious, you will probably be familiar with the likes of Hitchens, Dawkins, Harris and Dennett, known in the right circles as the Four Horsemen. You will also be familiar with the idea, which I first heard from the sceptic Michael Shermer but which they jointly espouse, that we are all atheists about 999 gods and that some of us just take it one god further.

At first glance this appears to be little more than a clever, somewhat witty remark. But it hides a deeper truth.

The current estimation is that there have been around a thousand religions throughout what we know of man's story. The vast majority of these religions have faded into oblivion; known only to history. We need not count a handful of people in the modern world who have adopted an otherwise defunct religion for their own reasons, which usually have little to do with a genuine belief in the old gods and certainly does not reflect any continuity of belief.

As example, for modern monotheists, neither the Norse panoply of gods nor the Greek or Roman pantheons are seen as contenders for the celestial throne, in opposition to the Judaeo-Christian God or the Islamic Allah. Nor does the Abrahamic God compete with Prajapati or the various aspects of Brahma in the Hindu faith or indeed the veneration of the Buddha. But the 999 old gods were once worshipped with all the fervour and certainty displayed by believers of the three monotheistic faiths today. Their followers were once equally sincere and equally certain.

With an arrogance typical of monotheists, the followers of Abraham's God claim that belief in these older deities faded in the face of their 'true' faith and that the dominance of their god proves that he exists whilst all the others were merely inventions. This is an overly simplistic idea and has been discredited in many ways but the purpose here is not to delve into that particular controversy. Rather, it is a brief synopsis of how belief in these gods may have evolved and how it then changed into a conviction that, in the words of the Highlander, Connor MacLeod, *"there can be only one"*.

There is a bewildering variety of myths regarding the creation of the world and of man and they cannot all be correct. Worshippers of the Abrahamic God are raised with the story of Adam & Eve in a garden and all other myths seem laughable but in truth the only difference is our familiarity. Unfortunately, despite such sincere belief in Adam & Eve and all things biblical, there is no evidence to demonstrate that any one of them is more likely than any other. So, we may leave myth aside for the moment and focus on what we may surmise was in the minds of our earliest human ancestors.

Surrounded by so much they could not understand and yet possessed of the insatiable curiosity and capacity for abstract thought which, together, distinguishes us from the rest of animal kingdom, it is highly probable that they attributed spirits to everything around them in order to explain the mysterious. Indeed, even today there are animist religions which do just that. Did the mountain explode into fire? Then the fiery mountain spirit must be angry. Did the river flood and wash away the wild rice? Then the river was displeased. It is in our nature to assign agency to things we do not understand. Indeed, without better information with which to explain the mysterious, it is a logical path.

Once we have assigned human thinking and emotion to a spirit, the next obvious step, in a hostile and unforgiving world, is to seek to establish some measure of control. The river is clearly angry with us and that's why it washed away our food source. We must give a gift to the river to placate it and that gift should logically be something valuable, such as some of our precious food. That didn't work, so clearly, we have not done enough. Perhaps a human sacrifice? The terrible thing about such thinking is that a failure need not be attributable to the spirit of the river but to insufficient propitiation. If our tribute didn't work, *we* failed therefore *we* must do more. In that way, what begins as a simple offering eventually and with a terrible irresistible logic, becomes the sacrifice of children and cutting the hearts from living enemies.

Once such a belief structure is in place, it is easy to see how the various animistic spirits might be resolved into something more distant from the world itself. Perhaps the spirit of our river and the river spirit of the tribe in the next valley are not separate. Perhaps there is an overall spirit, or god, of all rivers. And so, as mankind became more numerous and more settled into societies with shared cultures, the gods evolved with us, into things at once more sophisticated and more familiar.

Clearly the gods are not all good, nor all bad. Sometimes they help, sometimes they hinder. Sometimes they can be placated, other times they bring destruction or disease. So how to understand the nature of the gods? Well, what examples do we have? We can see that men are also sometimes bad and sometimes good. It seems clear then that the gods must be like us, only more so. Perhaps, that is even *why* men behave so. The gods then may be seen as men writ large.

It is easy to see how the idea of multiple deities would arise and how belief in them would not falter, despite the fact that they are often malicious, or at the very least, capricious. The cooperation of the gods cannot be guaranteed but it is still worthwhile worshipping and making offerings to them. Things aren't great now but how much worse could the gods make it?

From that point, a further evolution, from a pantheon to a single God, was probably inevitable. With same line of reasoning that took us from many river spirits to a god of all rivers, we might ask why must there be lots of gods? Gods are very obviously far above men and not governed by the rules and customs of our

societies. The world must have had a cause and that cause is unlikely to have been the over complicated explanation of our ancestors, replete with the actions of primeval animals or a god giving birth or cutting bits off another. Far more likely is the notion that it was a single incredible act by a single prime mover. Maybe, the gods answer to a higher power, just as we answer to them. Or maybe the gods are not individuals, competing against one another. Maybe, they are simply different aspects of a single creator. Hinduism, despite its apparent bewildering variety, retains this belief, that all the gods are manifestations or avatars of Brahman and we can see that it is a logical progression which explains monotheism.
Spirits of a place or event become many gods, become many aspects of one god, becomes a single creator, amused by the stumbling and mistaken ideas of previous generations and now revealed in all his glory.

So, we can understand how belief in a single God may have arisen. But such belief is problematic in that at no point does such belief require that the spirits, gods or God are real, only that they are believed to be. There is absolutely no empirical evidence for any religious belief and all of them, regardless of the details, may be considered to have the same potential of being true or false. Where they differ is in how we may logically explain their attraction.

Take the Greek pantheon as an example. It is easy to see how belief in the gods may have evolved. It is also easy to see how the relationship men had with their gods could be sustained. If you expect only that your gods will behave in the same way as men, but with far greater power and consequence, you are free to worship as it suits and to argue with the gods or even deny them as circumstances dictate. Such freedom is more difficult in monotheism. It is interesting that the first widespread monotheistic faith, Judaism, is far more comfortable with the notion of arguing with their God than is the later Christianity or

Islam, both of whom have developed the concept of blasphemy to such a degree as to punish any questioning of their tenets or any straying from orthodoxy. We should ask whether it is God or the priesthood who are most threatened by blasphemy.

We must keep in mind that worshipping any deity requires faith. That is, belief without evidence. Indeed, the concept of questioning or challenging belief in God is of such concern to Christianity and Islam that both religions promote faith itself as a virtue and, as a direct consequence, a lack of faith as a crime against God. Both religions have injunctions against relying on one's own thinking.

Because of the lack of evidence, all religions are equally likely to be true or false. We are then left with a situation where such belief in gods, as men writ large, is perfectly understandable but that belief in a single God, which by its very nature is perfect; omniscient, omnipresent and all-powerful, requires a far greater depth of belief; far more faith. When something bad happens to a follower of Apollo, it requires no alteration in the follower's beliefs because he already knows Apollo can be difficult. But if a follower of a single, loving God loses a child to illness or sees his city destroyed by natural disaster or by the followers of a different god, how is this to be explained?

The answer, of course, is that it cannot. Believers resort to trite responses to explain the unexplainable. *"God works in mysterious ways"*. *"It is not given to us to understand God's plan"*. *"It is the will of Allah"*. All of these reveal a serious problem that must be resolved for the believer if belief is to continue but for which there is no real answer. If God loves us, why does bad stuff keep happening? Equally, references to free will and God's promise not to interfere in the affairs of men again, are fraught with difficulties which believers can only answer with a declaration of faith.

Ultimately, it is easy to explain the how's and why's of belief in the old multiple gods. Far harder though to explain why people in the modern world still cling to their belief in a bronze-age single God. Part of the answer lies in the comfort such belief offers. Part lies in the strength of childhood conditioning and confirmation bias. But a significant part also lies in the fact that most people of faith have a poor grasp of the finer details and the history of their religion. For example, numerous studies have shown how few Christians regularly read their Bible or attend church. Christians and even Muslims (who are expected to read parts of their holy book daily, or be read to) have an incomplete knowledge of their religion and cherry pick the parts which they choose to follow. In this way, they are not challenged by what they believe. They are not called upon to think deeply about what they believe and are never called upon to justify it.

Is it more logical to believe in multiple gods? Not really. We may better understand such belief but that understanding itself precludes the ability to believe.
So, is monotheism a superior alternative? Hardly. The truth is that belief in such an invisible and difficult to understand deity is inconceivable without blind faith. Without a willingness to accept the teaching of your religion without question. Indeed, without the view that faith itself is a virtue that supersedes the accumulation of knowledge. Consider; modern believers in the God of Abraham are happy to take advantage of the marvels of the modern world but they base their personal worldview on an ideology formulated many centuries ago. Any change in this world view is not just unwelcome but impossible. And they do not see the dichotomy.

If you accept religion as your reason for living, then critical thinking, rationalism and logic have no place in your worldview. That is not to say that religious people are stupid. There are a great many highly intelligent and rational people who believe but in order to do so they must apply different rules to their thinking and actions about their religion than they do to every other part of their lives. There are even a small number of scientists who are people of faith. They apply rigorous analysis and logic to their work and require clear, unambiguous observable and repeatable evidence for everything they do but, in a remarkable application of double standards, they excuse their belief in God from such rigour. When questioning how such smart people can do this, it is not uncommon to hear someone say, *"I understand the logic of everything you have said but I still believe"*. Such compartmentalised thinking is frustrating.

Ultimately, belief in a God or gods is a choice. We cannot directly choose to what to believe but we can choose whether we require evidence and apply critical thinking or blindly believe because it feels right. We can choose to seek evidence and to be sceptical if such evidence is consistently lacking. There is a quote I like, from an imaginary philosopher in a computer game,

"Beware he who would deny you access to information, for in his heart he dreams himself your master".

Compare that to Proverbs 3:5

"Trust in the LORD with all your heart; and lean not on your own understanding".

Religions tell us not to seek too many answers and that faith itself is a virtue. This alone should make us question why we are not supposed to ask.

As to whether a God or a pantheon of gods is the more logical, more likely option, I suppose it comes down to whose imaginary friend would win in a fight.

THE STORY OF NOAH

I will say at the outset that there can be absolutely no doubt that the story of Noah and the flood is just that, a story. A fiction. My, somewhat tongue-in-cheek, analysis is designed to highlight how preposterous the tale really is and to counter those that still claim the Bible to be the inerrant word of God.

For the vast majority of Christians and Jews, the magic of the Bible is found in the inspiration and comfort that they draw from it. My words are not aimed at them but at the literalists who claim the Bible is the inerrant word of God.

And so.............

Genesis 5.32. *And Noah was five hundred years old: and Noah begat Shem, Ham, and Japheth.*
I think we can safely leave aside biblical ages as being somewhat fanciful. Much like 'Here be dragons' on old maps.

6.1.6. *And it came to pass, when men began to multiply on the face of the earth, and daughters were born unto them, 6.2. That the sons of God saw the daughters of men that they were fair; and they took them wives of all which they chose. Sons of God and daughters of men.*
 This distinction between the offspring of God and of men is repeated. A strange reference if the author didn't truly believe that the sons of God were actually different from humans. We must therefore assume that he did.

6.3 *And the LORD said, My spirit shall not always strive with man, for that he also is flesh: yet his days shall be an hundred and twenty years.*
Noah would be the last to live for many centuries. In reality, 120 is still a highly unlikely age for people of that time. Perhaps the authors felt that their predecessors ate healthier and worked out.

6.4 *There were giants in the earth in those days; and also after that, when the sons of God came in unto the daughters of men, and they bore children to them, the same became mighty men which were of old, men of renown.*

It's a shame but this is probably not a reference to real giants but to 'men of renown'. But, if the Bible is truly the inerrant word of God, perhaps there really were giants. I like to think so.

6.5 And God saw that the wickedness of man was great in the earth, and that every imagination of the thoughts of his heart was only evil continually. 6.6 And it repented the LORD that he had made man on the earth, and it grieved him at his heart. 6.7 And the LORD said, I will destroy man whom I have created from the face of the earth; both man, and beast, and the creeping thing, and the fowls of the air; for it repenteth me that I have made them.

A problem here for all those who believe in a kind and loving God. Why destroy all life? If God is all-powerful and all-knowing, surely he could have merely willed man out of existence without all the fuss. I know you can't trust squirrels (they're plotting something) but what harm did the three-toed sloth do? Also, why didn't an omniscient god see it coming and act sooner, before global genocide was necessary?

6.8 But Noah found grace in the eyes of the LORD. 6.9 These are the generations of Noah: Noah was a just man and perfect in his generations, and Noah walked with God. 6.10 And Noah begat three sons, Shem, Ham, and Japheth. 6.11 The earth also was corrupt before God, and the earth was filled with violence. 6.12 And God looked upon the earth, and, behold, it was corrupt; for all flesh had corrupted his way upon the earth.

Repetition of an earlier section, which is typical of the Bible. Such repetitions are usually different in style and emphasis and demonstrate that it was not written by a single author. If numerous authors are accepted, albeit possibly inspired by God, it is clearly feasible that errors occurred.

6.13 And God said unto Noah, the end of all flesh is come before me; for the earth is filled with violence through them; and, behold, I will destroy them with the earth. 6.14 Make thee an ark of gopher wood;

rooms shalt thou make in the ark, and shalt pitch it within and without with pitch. 6.15 And this is the fashion which thou shalt make it of:
The length of the ark shall be three hundred cubits 475 feet or 146 metres, the breadth of it fifty cubits 79 feet or 24.5 metres, and the height of it thirty cubits 47.5 feet or14.5 metres.

A cubit, being the length of the arm from elbow to fingertip, was different in various places in the region. 19 inches can be taken as an average.

This was a vessel almost certainly larger than any the author had ever seen. Its description was probably meant to be impressive, by its size and by giving exact measurements. Impressive or not, it was clearly not big enough for its intended purpose.

6.16 A window shalt thou make to the ark, …
A window, just one.

… and in a cubit shalt thou finish it above; and the door of the ark shalt thou set in the side thereof; with lower, second, and three stories shalt thou make it.
Three decks and one small window? The smell must have been quite something. In fact, death by methane poisoning is virtually guaranteed in such a vessel filled with animals.

6.17 And, behold, I, even I, do bring a flood of waters upon the earth, to destroy all flesh, wherein is the breath of life, from under heaven; and every thing that is in the earth shall die.
Destroy all flesh. Everything shall die. Everything? Really? The word 'overkill' springs to mind. Seems like a temper tantrum. Someone definitely needed a hug.

6.18 But with thee will I establish my covenant; and thou shalt come into the ark, thou, and thy sons, and thy wife, and thy sons' wives with thee. 6.19 And of every living thing of all flesh, two of every sort shalt thou bring into the ark, to keep them alive with thee; they shall be male and female.

Did Noah need the gender thing spelling out?

6.20 Of fowls after their kind, and of cattle after their kind, of every creeping thing of the earth after his kind, two of every sort shall come unto thee, to keep them alive. 6.21 And take thou unto thee of all food that is eaten, and thou shalt gather it to thee; and it shall be for food for thee, and for them.

So, we have a good sized three decker by the standards of the day, but to hold two of <u>every</u> species and their food? It must have been a bit cramped and I don't want to think of all the mucking out. And how did they stop the polar bears from eating the seals? A miracle you say? Ah, I see.

6.22 Thus did Noah; according to all that God commanded him, so did he.

7.1 And the LORD said unto Noah, Come thou and all thy house into the ark; for thee have I seen righteous before me in this generation. 7.2 Of every clean beast thou shalt take to thee by sevens, the male and his female: and of beasts that are not clean by two, the male and his female. 7.3 Of fowls also of the air by sevens, the male and the female; to keep seed alive upon the face of all the earth. 7.4 For yet seven days, and I will cause it to rain upon the earth forty days and forty nights; and every living substance that I have made will I destroy from off the face of the earth.

So Noah had just one week to gather 2, or 7, of every species on earth. A tough job for 4 men and one of them 600 years old already and the three lads one hundred each. Even putting aside the trouble of loading predator and prey together, how did the animals get there from all around the earth in one week? The kangaroos must have struggled a bit but it's the penguins I feel sorry for, they have such little legs.

7.5 And Noah did according unto all that the LORD commanded him. 7.6 And Noah was six hundred years old when the flood of waters was upon the earth. 7.7 And Noah went in, and his sons, and his wife, and his sons' wives with him, into the ark, because of the waters of the flood. 7.8 Of clean beasts, and of beasts that are not clean, and of fowls, and of every thing that creepeth upon the earth, 7.9 There went in two and two unto Noah into the ark, the male and the female, as God had commanded Noah.

OK, so we're back to 2 by 2. Another hint at more than one version of the story?

7.10 And it came to pass after seven days, that the waters of the flood were upon the earth. 7.11 In the six hundredth year of Noah's life, in the second month, the seventeenth day of the month, …

Unusually and unnecessarily specific. Presumably to make it seem real.

… the same day were all the fountains of the great deep broken up, and the windows of heaven were opened.

This seems a simple statement but it betrays the primitive world view of the authors; a flat earth surrounded by water instead of space and covered by a solid firmament with windows to let the rain through, as in Gen 1.6-10.

7.12 And the rain was upon the earth forty days and forty nights. 7.13 In the selfsame day entered Noah, and Shem, and Ham, and Japheth, the sons of Noah, and Noah's wife, and the three wives of his sons with them, into the ark; 7.14 They, and every beast after his kind, and all the cattle after their kind, and every creeping thing that creepeth upon the earth after his kind, and every fowl after his kind, every bird of every sort.

The consensus conservative estimate of distinct species on earth today is 8.5 million! If the Bible is true and evolution is a myth, these must have existed in Noah's time. That seems like a lot on one boat.

7.15 And they went in unto Noah into the ark, two and two of all flesh, wherein is the breath of life. 7.16 And they that went in, went in male and female of all flesh, as God had commanded him …

2 by 2 again

… and the LORD shut him in. 7.17 And the flood was forty days upon the earth; and the waters increased, and bore up the ark, and it

was lift up above the earth. 7.18 And the waters prevailed, and were increased greatly upon the earth; and the ark went upon the face of the waters. 7.19 And the waters prevailed exceedingly upon the earth; and all the high hills, that were under the whole heaven, were covered. 7.20 Fifteen cubits upward did the waters prevail; and the mountains were covered.

Unless water behaved very differently back then and could cling to slopes to a depth of 15 cubits without pooling in the valleys, we must take this to mean that the tops of the mountains were covered by 15 cubits, [approx 24 feet, or 7 metres]. That depth, taking Everest as a guide, was 8,855 metres above the previous sea level, across the whole world! Keep in mind that water finds its own level and a truly global flood would have a uniform depth.

7.21 And all flesh died that moved upon the earth, both of fowl, and of cattle, and of beast, and of every creeping thing that creepeth upon the earth, and every man: 7.22 All in whose nostrils was the breath of life, of all that was in the dry land, died.

Again, a bit rough considering God was only angry with the humans.

7.23 And every living substance was destroyed which was upon the face of the ground, both man, and cattle, and the creeping things, and the fowl of the heaven; and they were destroyed from the earth: and Noah only remained alive, and they that were with him in the ark. 7.24 And the waters prevailed upon the earth an hundred and fifty days.

8.1 And God remembered Noah, and every living thing, and all the cattle that was with him in the ark: and God made a wind to pass over the earth, and the waters assuaged.

OK, so a wind dried up billions of tons of water across the whole earth. But wind is just air in motion, produced by the uneven heating of the earth's surface by the sun. For wind to dry up the water it must turn it to vapor and carry it away. But away to where? Where would the water be carried to and deposited in a global flood? Could it be that God didn't know how the wind was made?

8.2 *The fountains also of the deep and the windows of heaven were stopped, and the rain from heaven was restrained; 8.3 And the waters returned from off the earth continually: and after the end of the hundred and fifty days the waters were abated. 8.4 And the ark rested in the seventh month, on the seventeenth day of the month, upon the mountains of Ararat. 8.5 And the waters decreased continually until the tenth month: in the tenth month, on the first day of the month, were the tops of the mountains seen.*
Hang on. The ark landed on Ararat in the seventh month, but the tops of the mountains were not seen for another three months? Unless Ararat has shrunk a lot since then, this passage alone makes a nonsense of the whole tale.

8.6 *And it came to pass at the end of forty days, that Noah opened the window of the ark which he had made: 8.7 And he sent forth a raven, which went forth to and fro, until the waters were dried up from off the earth. 8.8 Also he sent forth a dove from him, to see if the waters were abated from off the face of the ground; 8.9 But the dove found no rest for the sole of her foot, and she returned unto him into the ark, for the waters were on the face of the whole earth: then he put forth his hand, and took her, and pulled her in unto him into the ark.*
A little confusing. Noah sends out his raven, which flies about until the waters have dried up. Then he sends out a dove which cannot find dry land. Was the raven still out there? The poor thing must have been exhausted.

8.10 *And he stayed yet other seven days; and again he sent forth the dove out of the ark; 8.11 And the dove came in to him in the evening; and, lo, in her mouth was an olive leaf plucked off: so Noah knew that the waters were abated from off the earth. 8.12 And he stayed yet other seven days; and sent forth the dove; which returned not again unto him any more.*
So, they had been on the boat for 150 days. They landed but

Noah waited another 40 days. Then he sent out a raven and waited 7 days. Then he sent a dove and waited 7 days and the dove came back with a leaf. Then he waited another 7 days and when the dove didn't come back only then did he know the water had gone. But the ark had already landed 61 days ago! We have all had holidays we didn't want to end but after almost 6 months at sea, he made his family wait another 2 months! I bet they loved him for that.

And it came to pass in the six hundredth and first year, in the first month, the first day of the month, …
More strangely and unnecessarily specific detail designed to sell the story

… the waters were dried up from off the earth: and Noah removed the covering of the ark, and looked, and, behold, the face of the ground was dry. 8.14 And in the second month, on the seven and twentieth day of the month, was the earth dried.
Just a moment. I'm confused. Genesis 8.4 says that the ark landed on the 17th of the seventh month. Now it's the 25th of the second month. Is it a new year, over seven months later?

It seems like it took just 40 days and nights to inundate the earth but up to 8 months for the earth to dry out. Sorry to be a little picky about physics here but where did the vast amount of water come from and to where did it go? The volume has been calculated as approx 4,525,000,000,000 cubic kilometres of water [See paper by Dr Marty Leipzig 09.02.99]

And God spake unto Noah, saying, 8.16 Go forth of the ark, thou, and thy wife, and thy sons, and thy sons' wives with thee. 8.17 Bring forth with thee every living thing that is with thee, of all flesh, both of fowl, and of cattle, and of every creeping thing that creepeth upon the earth; that they may breed abundantly in the earth, and be fruitful, and multiply upon the earth. 8.18 And Noah went forth, and his sons, and his wife, and his sons' wives with him: 8.19 Every beast, every creeping thing, and every fowl, and whatsoever creepeth upon the earth, after their kinds, went forth out of the ark. 8.20 And Noah builded an altar unto the LORD; and took of every clean beast, and of every clean fowl, and offered burnt offerings on the altar. 8.21 And the LORD smelled a sweet savour; and the LORD said in his heart, I will not again curse the ground any more for man's sake; for the imagination of man's heart is evil from his youth; neither will I again smite any more every thing living, as I have done. 8.22 While the earth remaineth, seedtime and harvest, and cold and heat, and summer and winter, and day and night shall not cease.

This is a huge change of heart. From rage fuelled genocide against all life on Earth to a thoughtful god who even seems to acknowledge that his wiping out of every living thing was a bit much. And just from smelling cooked meat? We all love barbecue but come on!

9.1 And God blessed Noah and his sons, and said unto them, Be fruitful, and multiply, and replenish the earth. 9.2 And the fear of you and the dread of you shall be upon every beast of the earth, and upon every fowl of the air, upon all that moveth upon the earth, and upon all the fishes of the sea; into your hand are they delivered. 9.3 Every moving thing that liveth shall be meat for you; even as the green herb have I given you all things.

Interesting. So, despite earlier references to clean animals, Noah and his descendants could eat <u>every</u> kind of living thing, not just the kosher ones? So why tell him to take seven of the clean animals?

9.49.4 But flesh with the life thereof, which is the blood thereof, shall ye not eat. 9.5 And surely your blood of your lives will I require; at the hand of every beast will I require it, and at the hand of man; at the hand of every man's brother will I require the life of man. 9.6 Whoso sheddeth man's blood, by man shall his blood be shed: for in the image of God made he man.

Considering there were only eight of them, all family, God's words here might actually be addressing the author's intended audience? Just a thought. And why the focus on requiring the blood of men? It all feels a bit dark. And that last part; *'in the image of God made he man'*, if it is God talking, who is the 'he' referring to?

9.7 And you, be ye fruitful, and multiply; bring forth abundantly in the earth, and multiply therein. 9.8 And God spake unto Noah, and to his sons with him, saying, 9.9 And I, behold, I establish my covenant with you, and with your seed after you; 9.10 And with every living creature that is with you, of the fowl, of the cattle, and of every beast of the earth with you; from all that go out of the ark, to every beast of the earth. 9.11 And I will establish my covenant with you, neither shall all flesh be cut off any more by the waters of a flood; neither shall there any more be a flood to destroy the earth. 9.12 And God said, This is the token of the covenant which I make between me and you and every living creature that is with you, for perpetual generations: 9.13 I do set my bow in the cloud, and it shall be for a token of a covenant between me and the earth. 9.14 And it shall come to pass, when I bring a cloud over the earth, that the bow shall be seen in the cloud: 9.15 And I will remember my covenant, which is between me and you and every living creature of all flesh; and the waters shall no more become a flood to destroy all flesh. 9.16 And the bow shall be in the cloud; and I will look upon it, that I may remember the everlasting covenant between God and every living creature of all flesh that is upon the earth.
Ah, that's nice. Who doesn't love a rainbow? But hold on a minute. An omniscient God needed a rainbow as a reminder not to destroy all life on earth again? Why? In case he had a bad hair day and just lashed out? And if the rainbow is the mark of God's covenant, are we to believe that prior to this there were no rainbows, no light refracted through raindrops?

9.17 And God said unto Noah, This is the token of the covenant, which I have established between me and all flesh that is upon the earth. 9.18 And the sons of Noah, that went forth of the ark, were Shem, and Ham, and Japheth: and Ham is the father of Canaan. 9.19 These are the three sons of Noah: and of them was the whole earth overspread

So, every human on earth is descended from Noah's three sons, regardless of race and geography and it all happened only 4000 years ago. How does that work?

9.20 And Noah began to be an husbandman, and he planted a vineyard: 9.21 And he drank of the wine, and was drunken; and he was uncovered within his tent. 9.22 And Ham, the father of Canaan, saw the nakedness of his father, and told his two brethren without. 9.23 And Shem and Japheth took a garment, and laid it upon both their shoulders, and went backward, and covered the nakedness of their father; and their faces were backward, and they saw not their father's nakedness. 9.24 And Noah awoke from his wine, and knew what his younger son had done unto him. 9.25 And he said, Cursed be Canaan; a servant of servants shall he be unto his brethren. 9.26 And he said, Blessed be the LORD God of Shem; and Canaan shall be his servant. 9.27 God shall enlarge Japheth, and he shall dwell in the tents of Shem; and Canaan shall be his servant.

Now, we have to talk about this.
Poor old Noah, probably a little senile at 600 years old, was naked in his own tent. So what? He was at home, relaxing and having a beer. Who cares? I think what happened next was a bit harsh. The two good sons only knew Noah was drunk and naked because their brother told them and he only told them because he was concerned. Now all his descendants are cursed to be slaves, servants of servants, the lowest of the low? Leaving aside the author's evident problem with nakedness, this might actually be a very poor way of justifying the oppression of the Canaanites by the author's people, especially as new archaeological and paleo-biology evidence demonstrates no clear distinctions of race or even culture between the various inhabitants of the region in Old Testament times.

And Noah lived after the flood three hundred and fifty years. 9.29 And all the days of Noah were nine hundred and fifty years: and he died.

Summary and Conclusions

Unless we read it purely from a position of blind faith, there is so much wrong with the story of Noah that it is hard to know where to begin. A modern interpretation is that it evolved from a local legend or legends, from a time when the people affected had no real knowledge of a world greater than their own valley. The legend was at some point incorporated into the verbal history of the Jewish people and, when the various books of the Bible were being collected, it was included and perhaps enhanced to reinforce the relationship between God and his chosen people. As with other parts of the Bible, there does appear to be at least two competing versions here. Possibly different oral traditions melded together by the authors.

It is important to understand that to people of a less informed age, the story would not have seemed unusual. Creation legends and supposedly historical myths abound from every part of the world. Direct communication with God, or with gods, was once commonly accepted. Even today, every race or group of humans; the tribes of the Amazon rain forest, Kalahari bushmen in Africa and Australian aboriginals, all have their own creation stories. Even more modern origin stories, such as how the USA came to be, are full of inaccuracies and often deliberate falsehoods, because they are not designed to be 'true', they are meant to fulfil a purpose.

Many biblical stories may be taken as allegory and any clear falsehoods or internal inconsistencies can thereby be safely ignored. In this case, however, it does seem that, by including very specific details, the authors of Noah's tale intended it to be taken literally. This creates problems for any modern believer, graced as we are with greater knowledge of our world and with tools with which to test ideas and stories.

It doesn't need a mathematician or a biologist to see that it would have been impossible for Noah and his family to collect representatives of every species that crawled, walked or flew, let alone gather them under one small roof in a week. And the work involved in throwing that much dung over the side every day doesn't bear thinking about. Add to that the subsequent spread of animals and humans to all parts of the earth and the whole story becomes silly. If we suspend our cynicism and stretch the bounds of probability beyond breaking point, we can perhaps accept the logic in saving penguins and kangaroos, but I can't help thinking that a species of bug, which burrows into children's eyeballs to lay eggs, only for the larvae to eat their way out again, leaving African children blind and in agony, could safely have been allowed to drown.

Modern day creationists try to be clever and refer to the word 'kind' in the story. They say that there didn't need to be two of every species, just two of every kind. For example, not two of every type of dog, just two ancestors of all dog-like creatures alive today. They use a biblical definition of 'kind', as creatures who can mate and produce viable (i.e. not sterile) offspring. Unfortunately for the literalists, this results in far more animals than is feasible. There have been a number of different interpretations offered by religious apologists regarding just how many animals were on the ark but the creationist organisation, Answers In Genesis, give the figure as 8,000 kinds, that is 16,000 individual creatures, plus 7 of each clean animal. It should be clear that keeping so many animals, together with their incredibly varied food requirements is clearly impossible on a vessel about the same size as a modern-day frigate. And keep in mind they had only one small window. And we haven't yet thought about the unimaginably vast numbers of insects with short life spans that could not have survived a global flood unaided, or the problems with fresh and salt water aquatic life. Oh, and the dinosaurs, let's not forget them. Answers In Genesis believe they were saved too and went extinct later.

The authors of the book of Genesis believed that the world was flat and that it existed within a sphere of water. The early verses of Genesis describe God parting the waters above from those below with a firmament he called Heaven and that the waters under heaven were collected to let dry land appear. Heaven was directly above the earth and water existed above heaven and below the earth (according to the story this is where the 4.5 billion cubic kilometres of water came from). The problem is that even the most ardent monotheist must acknowledge that this is simply nonsense.

In summary then:
An impossibly old man builds a boat which is just not big enough.
In one week, he gathers together representatives of _every_ animal on earth.
Billions of cubic kilometres of water appear from places that do not exist.
The whole world is covered with water 5.5 miles deeper than the initial sea level.
God sends a wind and the water goes back to the non-existent places it came from.
After what must have been an indescribably horrible 7.5 months spent feeding and cleaning up after the representatives of up to <u>8.5 million species</u> they come out into a cleansed world.
Herbivorous animals somehow manage to find food in this cleansed world and to fend of the starving predators for long enough spread to every corner of the globe.
Predatory animals, including humans, manage to find enough prey animals to live off, without destroying all the herbivores.
Three couples give rise to enough humans to re-populate the earth and divide into races as diverse as Eskimos and Pygmies, Chinese and Zulus.
This happened really quickly because the Bible makes it clear that, within the period of its writing, the middle east was occupied by Egyptians, Assyrians, Babylonians, Philistines etc. Remembering of course that the authors had no knowledge of

the world beyond.

And the family of Ham are cursed with slavery in perpetuity, simply for seeing his Dad naked.

Of course, it could have all been achieved by miracle. But if we accept that 'explanation' we would then also need to ascribe the development of all the varied human races and the vast diversity of life on earth to miracle, because in using this reasoning, evolution and species variation via natural selection is simply not allowed. I will not even get into that argument. It is possible to be so open minded that your brain falls out.

Finally, we need to place the flood in history. Luckily, using the calculations of Bishop Usher, accepted by believers in the unerring word of God as written in the Bible, we have an accurate timeline.

The world was created in 4,004 BC and is currently only 6,021 years old, at time of writing. The flood happened when the world was 1656 years old. This means that the flood occurred 4,365 years ago. The real problem with this can be shown best by an example. From a host of different sources, we know that the Pyramids of Giza were built between 2589 and 2504BC, that is about 4648 years ago. So, when the world was covered by the weight of 4.5 billion cubic kilometres of water to a depth of 5.5 miles, the pyramids were already 283 years old. It must have held essential maintenance back a bit and put the Pharaoh off his breakfast.

It is worth mentioning that we have Chinese documents from the same period recording details such as the passing of a comet and there were societies as far afield as India and Ireland creating art, pottery and writing. They were writing on stone because, presumably, paper would have been a bit soggy.

In the final analysis it is clear that we can discount the literal truth of whole Noah tale and accept that it is simply an entertaining part of the wonderful creation myth of the Hebrew people.

If you wish to believe it to be entirely true that is, of course, your choice. But, unless you can disprove any of the facts given above that run contrary to the story, you can only support your belief by use of miracle and unsubstantiated belief. The late Carl Sagan said, *"Extraordinary claims require extraordinary evidence"*. The rest of us are looking forward to reviewing your evidence.

NUMBERS 16

I have recently been asked to write a commentary on the main stories from the Old Testament, focussing on Genesis and Exodus. The idea is to highlight many of the impossibilities and plain weirdness and do so in a humorous way. The project will take time but in sketching out the basic framework it occurred to me that there is also a story in the book of Numbers which warrants discussion and is instructive in its own way. It will not be a part of the main work because there is absolutely nothing humorous in it.

Most people are familiar with the biblical account of the Exodus, where Moses leads the Israelites out of Egypt. At least, most people know the basics. But, as with so much of the Bible, it is the details that cause problems. The main problem is that the details show the god of the Israelites to be a deeply unpleasant and violent creature.
To demonstrate my meaning, let's take a look at the biblical account of a small incident on the Israelite's journey that is re-visited in the book of Numbers.

In Numbers 16, we read of a dispute in the Israelite camp. Korah of the Levites, the tribe with responsibility to look after the religious practices of the Israelites, approaches Moses with a complaint. With him are Dathan, Abiram and On, who were Reubenites and 250 leaders of the community. They speak to Moses and his brother Aaron, complaining that the two men are placing themselves above all others. Their main complaint is that the Levites are all holy men and so Moses and Aaron should not be in sole command.

As we might imagine, Moses doesn't take kindly to a challenge to his authority and he asks God for help. God, true to his nature as already shown in the Bible, helps in the way he knows best. He massacres people.

God first demands that Moses, Aaron and all the men that follow the complainers gather together, each with a bronze incense bowl to give praise to him. But this is only a trick. God gets Moses and Aaron to move everyone else away from the tents of the Levites and then the earth opens up and swallows them and closes over them. All the tents and the households, all the women and children and all their belongings, are gone in an instant. God then sends fire to consume the 250 men of the tribe who were, at that moment, busy offering tribute to him as they had been instructed, because they had a problem with Moses, not with God.

God's answer to people's complaints is not to assess whether the issue has merit, it is not to change the hearts and minds of the men or even to show his greatness and his favour for Moses in order to settle the matter. It is to murder them all along with their families. But this unpleasant little tale isn't over.

Despite the terrible fate of the complainants, the next day the whole congregation of the Israelites came to Moses and this time their complaint was that he had *"killed the Lord's people"*, because they clearly still believed in God. And what was God's response? More death of course. Here it is worth reading the actual passages, taken from the NIV translation (New International Version).

42 But when the assembly gathered in opposition to Moses and Aaron and turned toward the tent of meeting, suddenly the cloud covered it and the glory of the Lord appeared. 43 Then Moses and Aaron went to the front of the tent of meeting, 44 and the Lord said to Moses, 45 "Get away from this assembly so I can put an end to them at once." And they fell facedown.
46 Then Moses said to Aaron, "Take your censer and put incense in it, along with burning coals from the altar, and hurry to the assembly to make atonement for them. Wrath has come out from the Lord; the plague has started." 47 So Aaron did as Moses said, and ran into the midst of the assembly. The plague had already started among the people, but Aaron offered the incense and made atonement for them. 48 He stood between the living and the dead,

and the plague stopped. 49 But 14,700 people died from the plague, in addition to those who had died because of Korah. 50 Then Aaron returned to Moses at the entrance to the tent of meeting, for the plague had stopped.

It is worth thinking about this scene for a moment. Some leaders complained that Moses was getting above himself and God's reaction was to kill the leaders plus 250 men and all their families. When the whole of the Israelites complained about that, God sent a plague to wipe them out. God was so angry with the Israelite's challenge to Moses' authority that he was going to commit genocide, again. Aaron miraculously managed to stop the plague with some incense, which was clever of him but seems implausible, but nearly 15000 people died.

Consider. God sent Moses to bring his chosen people out from Egypt and to lead them to a promised land. Because they were ungrateful, he condemned them to wander in the desert for forty years. When some of them had a problem with Moses' attitude, God murdered 250 families. Then, to top it all, he decides to wipe out every single person he had previously saved. God was prevented from doing so by Aaron's quick thinking but he still managed to kill 14,700 people. Not for blasphemy, not for forging a golden idol or worshipping strange gods. For making a complaint.

Now, the story is clearly nonsense. We can be sure that none of it happened. From the lack of archaeological evidence and from the lack of a single Egyptian record mentioning a quarter of the population of Egypt just walking away, let alone the plagues and the death of all the firstborn of Egypt. Also, the idea that a million people could wander around lost for 40 years! in a desert the same size as West Virginia, or half the size of England, is just silly. And there is the small problem that, at the time mentioned in the Bible, we now know the promised land was inhabited by a number of small tribes or ethnic groups, all ruled by Egypt! The Israelites, it seems, fled Egypt to settle in Egyptian territory, after wiping out the people who presumably paid tribute to Egypt. But vast numbers of Jews and Christians believe it to be true in general and many believe it to be true in every detail because, to them, the Bible is the inerrant word of God.

Once again, we have to stop and think. Think about that fact that Christian literalists, who many of you probably know or have encountered, actually believe that the incident in Numbers 16 really happened. Moreover, they have no problem with it. They have no issue at all with the idea that their God, who they claim loves us, was pleased to kill 250 families for having a grumble and was prepared to wipe out all the Israelites, all of his chosen people, for daring to complain that Moses had been unfair. Is this a god worthy of worship?

Next time you meet one of these literalists, remind him or her of Numbers 16 and pay attention to the way they try to justify it. It will provide insight into their mindset and to what they think is right and proper.

MORALITY COMES FROM GOD

And the Ten Commandments

Religious believers and in particular religious leaders are at great pains to point out that mankind gets its moral sense from God. Moreover, they claim that our possession of moral values is evidence for the existence of God. I will make the case that far from being a gift from heaven, morality is inherent in all humans and can even be seen, if diluted, in other higher primates, such as Chimpanzees and Gorillas. This being so, it is not plausible to hold morality up as a proof for God's existence.

The greatest moral teaching in Judaeo-Christian tradition is, of course, the ten commandments. We are expected to believe that, after leading the Jews out of Egyptian captivity, Moses went up a mountain, communed with his maker and came back with God's moral code inscribed on tablets of stone, presumably to prove they were serious.

The Ten Commandments are held up as being the pinnacle of moral instruction and that without them we would be barbarous. Not only is this insulting to the Jews and all other nations, who had managed thus far without them, it is patent nonsense, as any quick scan of them will show. Let's take that scan now. I have used the King James version of the Bible, for no other reason than we can enjoy the language even if we disagree about the use to which it is employed.

I am the Lord your God, which have brought thee out of the land of Egypt, out of the house of bondage. Thou shalt have no other gods before me.
Thou shall not make unto thee any graven image, or any likeness of any thing that is in heaven above, or that is in the earth beneath, or that is in the water under the earth.
Thou shalt not bow down thyself to them; for I the Lord thy God am a jealous God, visiting the iniquity of the fathers upon the children unto the third and fourth generation of them that hate me. And shewing mercy unto thousands of them that love me and keep my commandments.
Thou shalt not take the name of the Lord thy God in vain, for the

Lord will not take him guiltless that taketh his name in vain.
Remember the Sabbath day to keep it holy. Six days shalt thou labour and do all thy work; but the seventh day is the Sabbath of the Lord thy God; in it thou shalt not do any work, thou, nor thy son, nor thy daughter, thy manservant, nor thy maidservant, nor thy cattle, nor the stranger that is within thy gates. For in six days the Lord made heaven and earth, the sea and all that is in them, and rested the seventh day; wherefore the Lord blessed the Sabbath day and hallowed it.
Honour thy father and thy mother; that thy days may be long upon the land which the Lord thy God giveth thee.
Thou shalt not kill.
Thou shalt not commit adultery.
Thou shalt not steal.
Thou shalt not bear false witness against thy neighbour.
Thou shalt not covet thy neighbour's house, thou shalt not covet thy neighbour's wife,
nor his manservant, nor his maidservant, nor his ox, nor his ass, nor any thing that is thy neighbour's.

The first thing that stares us in the face is that of the ten rules, only five of them are explicitly moralistic. The first four are only about how to worship God and the last is an injunction against what we may think; just in case you were under the impression that George Orwell invented the concept of 'thought crime' for his novel 1984.

  Let's take the commandments one at time and analyse them a little.

"I am the Lord your God…..Thou shalt have no other gods before me".
The first thing that strikes me here is that God is admitting the existence of other gods. Why else would he issue an instruction that he must come first? If he meant 'don't worship other gods because they are fiction', why not just say that?

So if, as believers claim, he is the one and only, what has happened to these others? But more disturbing for believers must be the question; if there are, or were, other gods, who actually created everything? If it was the Judeo-Christian God, why would he create rivals?

"Thou shall not make unto thee any graven image, or any likeness of any thing that is in
heaven above, or that is in the earth beneath, or that is in the water under the earth.
Thou shalt not bow down thyself to them; for I the Lord thy God am a jealous God, visiting
the iniquity of the fathers upon the children unto the third and fourth generation of them
that hate me. And shewing mercy unto thousands of them that love me and keep my
commandments".

There are two distinct parts to this commandment that should be addressed separately.
Firstly, we have a rule that no images are to be made. The Jewish and Islamic traditions are that no images of living creatures may used in a religious setting but this goes much further. In specifying no images of anything in the sky, on earth or in the water, God is very clear. This means that every sculptor, engraver and painter that ever lived is a sinner. And all the churches with stained glass windows are anathema. However, I think we can safely ignore it because in the text the real author, who we may presume is not God, betrays his primitive understanding of the world when he mentions the waters that are under the earth. This goes back to the description in Genesis, a careful reading of which will show it is nonsense but demonstrated the extent of worldly knowledge at that time.

The second part of this commandment is far more troubling. In ordering that the Jews must not worship graven images, God is not satisfied with a simple threat to the potential offenders.

He makes it clear that their children, grandchildren and great grandchildren will also be punished. A jealous god indeed. Had this been the words of Zeus we could accept it, as the Greek and Roman gods displayed all the human virtues and vices writ large, but such vehemence makes little sense for a supposed supreme being who created everything, already knows our hearts and minds and who rules alone. We might also question the morality of punishing generations as yet unborn for the crimes of their forebears. A terrible threat, no doubt, but hardly what we should expect from a loving father.

"Thou shalt not take the name of the Lord they God in vain, for the Lord will not take him guiltless
that taketh his name in vain"

.

Fair enough. A god's got have some rules I suppose.

"Remember the Sabbath day to keep it holy. Six days shalt thou labour and do all thy work; but the
seventh day is the Sabbath of the Lord thy God; in it thou shalt not do any work, thou, nor thy son,
nor thy daughter, thy manservant, nor thy maidservant, nor thy cattle, nor the stranger that is
within thy gates. For in six days the Lord made heaven and earth, the sea and all that is in them,
and rested the seventh day; wherefore the Lord blessed the Sabbath day and hallowed it".

The author, or God if you like, goes a long way around to say it but this is just about resting on the Sabbath. Note, however, that it makes no rule about worshipping, only taking the day off. The only small thing I could say about this is to question the idea that an all-powerful god would need to rest. Does this simple idea betray human origins? It is interesting to note that anyone who uses a horse to get to church on Sunday is committing a sin. Except that for the Jews, to whom this was written, the Sabbath is a Saturday.

Now we come to rules 5 through 9. These *are* about morals and we can have no objection to them, other than to suggest that the list should be much longer, if it were truly the guide for mankind it is supposed to be.

"Honour thy father and thy mother; that thy days may be long upon the land which the Lord thy
God giveth thee".
"Thou shalt not kill". **(**a more accurate translation is thou shalt not commit murder**)**
"Thou shalt not commit adultery".
"Thou shalt not steal".
"Thou shalt not bear false witness against thy neighbour".

A brief side note here to point out that Jesus seemed not to care about the injunction to honour one's father and mother because he ordered his followers to hate and abandon their parents.

And finally,
"Thou shalt not covet thy neighbour's house, thou shalt not covet thy neighbour's wife, nor his
manservant, nor his maidservant, nor his ox, nor his ass, nor any thing that is thy neighbour's".

This last commandment seems, on the surface, to be straightforward and not really open to criticism, but there is something very disturbing beneath that placid surface.
As mentioned previously, this is enshrining the notion of 'thought crime' into religious law. Now you can not only be punished for what you do, but for what you think. Coveting isn't doing, it is just a fancy word for wanting. If I am envious of my neighbour's posh house, I am committing a sin. If I lie in bed and wish his prize ox would wander into my field so I can use its strength to pull my plough, I am committing a sin, even if I never do anything about it. But more than that; without a little coveting, there would be no striving to better one's situation. No

working hard to buy the kids new shoes.

If you believe in God, you believe that he created everything, that he is all knowing and that he is all powerful. In other words, he made you, he already knows what's in your mind and he can crush you for what you're thinking. Think about that. Even though he is perfect and supposedly created you in His image, he quite deliberately created you flawed and he will still punish you for those very flaws. The late Christopher Hitchens put it well (paraphrasing Fulke Greville, a poet of the early seventeenth century)

"Created sick we are commanded to be well".

What awful tyranny is this, that we can be punished for the very nature we were given and for which we have no choice?

So, we can clearly see that the ten commandments are not the moral 'be all and end all'. In fact, even the five rules that are about morals are nothing more than simple common sense for anyone wishing to live in society with others. To imagine that mankind went through thousands of years not knowing these rules before Moses came down the mountain is lunacy. But what about the more general idea that we get our morals from God, a view which is shared by the Islamic religion?

The first thing to define is what we mean when making such a statement. If we simply mean that God created us and therefore gave us our moral code, in-built as it were, we are really not saying anything profound. To accept that, we must first accept the idea of God the creator, but there are many millions who do not accept the Judaeo-Christian God, but who still possess an equal level of morality. If we believe these people too were created by God but are simply mistaken, we must ask why God would allow the greater part of the human race to ignore him.

If, on the other hand, if we mean that we obtain our morals thorough the word of God, passed to us through holy writings, we are left in an even more difficult position. The Bible is not a moral book. In it, God orders genocide, condones slavery, praises the handing over of daughters for rape in order to protect strangers, orders the sacrifice of Abraham's first born as a test of faith, allows the torture of poor old Job for a similar reason, wipes out all life on earth because he is upset with mankind, promises the Israelites a new home but neglects to mention that a little genocide will be required before they can move in and a host of other terrible things. With the exception of personal revelation, which cannot be verified and therefore cannot be trusted, the only authority we have for the word of God is the Bible. Jewish and Christian religious leaders may have invented various rules over the years but they rest their own authority on the Bible. This being so, how can mankind possibly have obtained a moral code from such an immoral source? The same may be said of the Quran, which combines instructions for love and harmony with orders to kill non-believers.

In the final analysis it is simple common sense that mankind, in every part of the world and for many thousands of years, has applied morals as a way of living together in extended groups without wiping itself out. It is also important to realise that morals can change with societal norms. In the West we think it depraved to have sex with pre-teens and marriage is not permitted until age eighteen. But this is not so in other parts of the world and was not the case in the West until fairly recently. And yet our predecessors in Europe and the inhabitants of other parts of the globe were and are still moral in many other ways that we recognise.

Some Native American tribes did not see theft as wrong but as a way of proving one's courage. Until quite recently there were cannibals, who killed and ate their enemies in order to absorb their power; they would have baffled by any idea that such behaviour is wrong. These groups share many morals with us but in these key areas they differ markedly, so how can there be an objective morality? The Prophet Mohammed married a 6 year old when he was fifty and had sex with her when she turned 9. An act of paedophilia, disgusting to us today but it went unremarked because it was probably not so unusual at the time.

Morality is an inherent part of human nature and may be put down to ideas that are necessary for common existence. No child needs to be taught the golden rule; don't do to others what you would not wish done to you. As soon as children become aware of the sense of self and the fact that other things and people around them do not necessarily think and feel the same, they instinctively grasp that fundamental principal, even if they sometimes need to be reminded.

Morality does not come from God and, considering what we know of him from his holy books, we should be thankful for it.

IS ISLAM EVIL?

The question is bound to cause strong feelings, both for and against. I can already hear the cries of racist, Islamophobe and hate-monger. But in today's climate of world-wide unrest and violence associated with Muslim extremism, it is not an unreasonable question.

Let me begin by stating my position regarding religion in general. Although I was once an adherent of a major religion, after many years of thought and research I came to the conclusion that gods were created in man's image and not the other way around. I am a Humanist, committed to being 'good without God' and I see no need for believing in divine intervention in the creation or managing of the universe, other than the comfort it may bring to those contemplating death. Indeed, I feel that those who claim to understand and explain God, hold an impossible position when faced with questions about cancer in children, parasites which bury themselves into eyes causing blindness, natural disasters etc. There are a host of other scenarios.

Another point I wish to make clear is that whilst all religions are, in my view, equally wrong, they are not all equal in their effect. Compare a Muslim or Christian extremist with a Jain. Jains are the ultimate pacifists and preservers of life. As Sam Harris, the neuroscientist, pointed out, the more extreme a Jain becomes, the less we have to worry about him. Truly committed Jains drink though a cloth to avoid inadvertently swallowing and killing any bugs.

And so, to Islam.

The late great Christopher Hitchens was once asked whether he called his book God Is Not Great, in direct response to the Islamic mantra Allahu Akbar, usually rendered as God is Great, (*a more accurate translation is God is greater or God is the greatest*). He confirmed the assumption and said that, whilst the book was a polemic against all religion, Islam was the most dangerous religion. As may be imagined, he answered at some length but he prefaced his reply by saying that whilst he considered Islam to be the most dangerous religion at that time, had he been asked the question in the nineteen thirties and forties he would have placed Roman Catholicism as the most dangerous religion because of its refusal to condemn, and in many cases its alliance with, fascism. The same may also have been asserted at earlier points in Christian history. That was, of course, before the rise of the modern Islamic fundamentalist, terrorists and suicide bombers. Before Al Qaeda, Hamas, Boko Haram and ISIS.

A popular excuse, often used by Muslims and even more often by western apologists for Islam, is that the crimes and horrors attributed to people such as those groups mentioned above are the misguided actions of individual criminals and must not be used to judge Islam. Indeed, there is an increasing movement to have Islam called 'the religion of peace'. In the light of what we see almost daily around the world, trying to get such an idea and title universally accepted is a massive task.

The point is that religion cannot be analysed in isolation, by using the excuse that crimes committed in the name of religion are solely the fault of individuals and not the religion itself. If the tenets of that religion are themselves violent or so open to violent interpretation that no deity would allow them unless it was deliberate, then the religion itself is culpable.

Islam, according to its holy books and its teachers, is not just any testament and Mohammed not just any prophet. Both are the ultimate in their truth and the very last. God has spoken his final will, in Arabic. All must obey or suffer. To even think that there may be future revelations is blasphemy.

Let's think about that for a moment. Consider that Judaism awaits a messiah both spiritual and earthly, to rescue the chosen people, once they are finally worthy. Christians believe that the messiah has already been once and will come again to usher in God's kingdom on earth and choose those who will be 'saved'. But according to Islam and its over 1.7 billion followers (*figure from a 2021 survey but as Muslims have the highest fertility rate world-wide, the true figure is certainly higher*) all Jews and Christians are misguided, at best, and blasphemers to be persecuted, at worst. Islam allows no personal choice, no wavering. Mohammed was the very last prophet and the Quran is the final word of God, dictated in perfect Arabic by the angel Gabriel. To not obey is to deny the will of God.

If Islam preached nothing but love, kindness, understanding and tolerance, such a rigid stance would be nothing to concern us, but this is not the case. The Quran actually instructs Muslims to use violence. One estimate cites well over one hundred calls for violence against non-believers in the Quran. To be sure there are also calls for peace and love and it is true that there are more mentions of violence in the Bible than in the Quran, but there is a crucial difference. Whether one believes in it or not, the Bible is written as a history and its references to violence are limited to a fixed point in time. The Quran, conversely, is open ended and reads as an instruction manual for life today and every day. This is what allows a minority of Muslims to justify their violence and many more to refuse to condemn such action. They do not need to 'misinterpret' or misunderstand the text. The exhortation to fight and kill are written plainly. And those who claim that Jihad should be taken as an internal struggle for goodness, must justify not only the modern-day Islamic terrorists but also the spread of Islam through conquests by Mohammed and his successors.

To emphasise this point I would refer to a recent You Tube video of Sheik Assim al-Hakkem, a well respected Muslim scholar with over half a million online followers, in which he states clearly that Islam is at peace with the West only because it is not yet strong enough but in 40 or 50 years, the war will begin and the whole world will be conquered and enslaved.

So, what we are presented with is veneration and adherence to the text of a holy book which commands both total obedience and violence. The same teachings say that this book is God's final word and all must hear and obey. By Islam's own rules we cannot fudge matters by citing human translation error or simple mistakes. Allah will not allow such things. All copies of the Quran, at least those written in Arabic by Muslim scholars, are without error because God will not permit them to be otherwise.

Our problem, therefore, as has been pointed out by others, is not with bad people but with bad ideology.

Of course, there are many different types of Muslim. They range from the fanatic to the secular with every shade in between. It must be made clear that the vast majority want nothing more than to live productive lives in peace, surrounded by loving family. But at its core, Islam will not allow such backsliding. Peaceful, integrated, modern Muslims live in a way which breaks many of the religion's rules and the Islamic fundamentalists are absolutely right to criticise them. Islam is a fundamentalist religion. It brooks no interpretation, no softening, no accommodation with the changing world, no acceptance of non-Muslim neighbours. The Quran is explicit when it calls Muslims who will not fight for the faith hypocrites.

Shaykh Abdal Hakim Murad is a British Muslim who trains Imams for British mosques. He once said,
"Moderate Islam? Do not be an extreme Muslim; be extremely Muslim".

At first glance this seems a reasonable and smart thing to say but to be extremely Muslim it is necessary to not only believe the Quran to be the inerrant word of God but to follow the examples of the prophet Mohammed, as laid down in the Hadiths (sayings of the prophet) and the Sira (the biography of the prophet). Unfortunately, these do not provide a purely peaceful loving ideology.

And so we return to the original question, is Islam evil?

The term evil means more than just bad, it is filled with religious connotation and may, perhaps, be the wrong word. But is Islam dangerous? Undoubtedly. Is Islam inimical to life in the modern world. Certainly.

To put it into perspective, if Sheik Assim al-Hakeem is correct, then moderate Muslims will not be allowed to sit quietly. Once the war begins and fundamentalism takes over, the first requirement will be that all Muslims demonstrate their commitment and we have seen many times what happens to moderates who do not follow the will of fundamentalists.

In the 21st century we are moving, albeit desperately slowly, towards a greater understanding and acceptance of others. We still have a long way to go but in most countries around the world we are at least making the first steps towards goals of equality and justice. Only in the most under-developed and in particular the most Muslim countries do regimes still hold to the barbarous treatment of women, homosexuals and people of different colour, tribe or faith.

For the rest of us, whilst we may still be embarrassed by small-minded people in our midst clinging to outmoded ideas, we can at least see our failings and understand the mistakes in our history and our old ideas. We are working towards a better world.

Where the rest of the non-Muslim world has laws created by men for the purposes of better government, however flawed it often is, Muslims have only Sharia. The word means law but it is nothing like what the rest of us mean by the idea. In Sharia there are no concepts of equality or freedom, or justice, only the will of God, as interpreted by men of course. Muslims are told to obey the laws of the land as far as possible but their overriding commitment must be to Sharia and where that conflicts with man's laws, the will of God is all that is important, because to be a Muslim is to be a willing slave to Allah. Islam literally means submission and Muslim stems from an Arabic word meaning one who submits to God.

Islam does not want the better world the rest of us strive for. Indeed, it will not allow it. Islam, at its core, sees the society created by Mohammed in the desert of 630AD as the ideal. Moreover, whilst the Quran speaks only of fighting to defend the faith and specifically against pagans and idolators, in practice Islam places all non-Muslims into one of these groups and scholars today and throughout history have demanded that all Muslims fight to spread Islam and either subjugate non-believers or kill them, to ensure this ideal world is brought about. Peaceful Muslims who live and work in the West know this to be true even if they shy away from it in embarrassment.

Is Islam evil? I'm not sure how the word should be defined or used in modern parlance. As an ideology it is certainly dangerously flawed and only by ignoring its more stringent texts do the majority of Muslims refrain from warring on their neighbours or manage to live in the modern world at all.
I believe, like Hitchens, that Islam is the most dangerous threat we face. I must stress here that I refer specifically to the ideology and certainly not to all Muslims, but we cannot afford to shy away from the problem because we embrace political correctness or fear accusations of racism etc. The first step to resolving any problem is its identification. Let us be careful with our words and actions. Let us not condemn people because of ideology. Let us not be prompted by fear and suspicion into hatred. But let us not make the potentially fatal mistake of pretending the problem does not exist.

CAN WE TRUST THE GOSPELS?

Many Christians rely upon scripture and many even believe the Bible to be inspired by God, or even to be the inerrant word of God. But these beliefs are incredibly difficult to justify.

The problem with relying upon the scriptures is that we have no idea what the original manuscripts actually said. There are a great many scraps of early manuscript which are parts of one gospel or another but none of them may be relied upon to be an original and most are in poor condition. The earliest useable gospel we possess is a copy of Mark written around 150 years after the events it describes. The first 3 verses are missing, as are the last 4 and significant sections of text all the way through. There is an earlier scrap of John but it is only a part of a few lines, about the size of a credit card and tells us nothing of value.

What follows is a bullet pointed list to explain why the New Testament is not reliable.

- The gospels were not written and do not claim to be written by eyewitnesses.
- They are written in Educated Greek, a language unlikely to have been spoken by Jesus or his predominantly working-class followers.
- They were written between 30 and 100 years after the events they describe, by people probably living in Asia Minor who only knew of Jesus through oral stories.
- They differ markedly in many significant details and in the way they portray Jesus.
- The original books of the New Testament were handwritten and the only way to copy these was also by hand.
- All long manuscripts copied by hand have mistakes.
- As the books spread there were copies of copies, each likely to have mistakes. Then copies of copies of copies, with even more mistakes.
- We have many manuscripts of the gospels, made by trained monks, that are nonetheless full of errors large

and small, with missing words and paragraphs and even missing whole pages.

- The earliest copies of copies were not done by trained copyists but by ordinary people.
- The Bible was then translated into Latin, with yet more mistakes.
- We now have fragments or complete copies of 5,700 manuscripts and there are thousands of differences, some tiny, some substantial.
- There are also copies in various languages and as words do not always have direct translations, these copies make their own subtle changes.
- The earliest copy of the gospel of Mark we possess is from AD 200, some 150 years of hand copying after the original was written.
- The oldest fragment of the New Testament we possess is the credit card sized piece of John 15 mentioned above. It is dated, by palaeography, to AD125, plus or minus 25 years. Probably thirty or forty years after the original.
- We have no complete copy of John until one written around AD 200.
- We only have a few scraps and pieces of manuscript of the gospels from before AD 200.
- We only get multiple copies of the gospels from around AD 600-700.
- The best evidence we have comes from documents written at least 125 years after the originals were created and are the end of a chain of copies.
- How many copies there were, prior to the ones we have, is impossible to know. It is also impossible to know what the original versions actually said.

The vast majority of people in biblical times were far less literate than today and it is likely that even more errors would have occurred than would happen if we did a modern copy by hand. In addition, we can see, from later texts, where copyists have tried to correct what they thought were errors, but with no original to guide them. They then inserted text which is different from what we find in other manuscripts.

We do not have a complete copy of Mark, or any gospel, until the middle of the fourth century. 300 hundred years after Jesus. That is 300 hundred years of copying before we get a complete gospel. And it is worth repeating that the earliest copies were not made by educated monks in a dedicated environment set aside for the purpose but by ordinary individuals. These people, whilst no doubt sincere, were probably of varying abilities, not to mention possessing various different traditions and ideas of Jesus, which may be seen from Paul's letter to the various churches.

We have 5700 copies of the New Testament. Some more complete than others.
The vast majority of the New Testament manuscripts are from after the 9th century. All of them were hand copied. Imagine how many errors can occur through hand copying in eight or nine hundred years.

When we compare the gospel manuscripts, we find lots of mistakes. Most of them are trivial and very obviously what we would call typos today. These we may dismiss as unimportant. But there are others.

In 1707, John Mill, a scholar at Oxford, decided to write a new and authoritative version of the New Testament. He studied 100 Greek manuscripts and noted the differences he found. He then printed the New Testament, one paragraph at a time, with the various versions listed underneath. He noted and published 30,000 differences.

30,000 differences in 100 copies.
We now have 5700 copies. No-one has yet done a similar analysis to John Mill but the results would almost certainly be

staggering. But whichever text we may choose to believe is the more accurate, there are more differences than there are words in the New Testament.

But how many differences were there in the early manuscripts?

Accidental Changes

Most of the differences found are unimportant. They simply demonstrate that some scribes couldn't spell and that mistakes were made. We also have examples of where a scribe has missed a word, a line and even a whole page, presumably by accidently turning over two pages of the original and being so focussed on copying word by word that the error went unnoticed. There other examples where a word or a line has been written twice. These are easily explained and are not significant, other than to show that the whole idea of a reliable text is unsupportable.

Something noted above bears repeating. By the Middle Ages, copies were made by highly literate monks who specialised in copying important and holy books. And they still made a great many errors. In the very early years of Christianity, copies were made simply by people who wanted a copy, or by a scribe employed for that purpose. Therefore, the missing manuscripts from that time almost certainly had far more mistakes than later ones. How many we cannot know because the manuscripts that survive from that time are too fragmented, with huge sections lost to time or are only tiny scraps themselves but we should keep in mind that the later copies, with their own errors, were not copied from a perfect original but from those earlier imperfect attempts.

Deliberate changes

In addition to all the human error that has occurred over the centuries, there are also examples of where something was deliberately changed in a biblical manuscript. It must be said that whilst this happened a lot in the Old Testament manuscripts, it is rare for the New Testament but not unheard of. The best example of this is at John 5:7, where the earlier Greek manuscripts do not have the verse but the later Latin ones do.

"For there are three that bear record in heaven, the Father, the Word, and the Holy Ghost: and these three are one".

This is the only time in the whole Bible where the Trinity is described as three in one, rather than three separate entities. It is important because it forms a significant tenet of the Catholic church and yet has been proven to be a later addition. This is hard for literalists to accept because it entails changing, or adding to, words that were supposedly written by God or at the very least by special men inspired by God.

Internal Discrepancies

There are many places in the gospels where one account differs from another. As it is widely accepted today that the authors were not eyewitnesses, this is hardly unusual (the names we use for the authors were absent from early copies and were added later). However, as it is also accepted that Mark was the first gospel and that the gospels of Mathew and Luke contain 90% of what we find in Mark, word for word, with the authors simply adding their own ideas, it is a little strange that there are so many differences.

It is not feasible to list all of the differences here but as the crucifixion and resurrection is the very key to Christianity, I will give a few examples from that story. There are a great many more.

Who carried the cross?
Mark says the Romans grabbed Simon of Cyrene and made him carry it but John states that Jesus carried his own cross. John is keen to portray Jesus as God and so he wouldn't have needed help.

What were Jesus' last words?

This might be seen as vitally important and yet the gospels give three totally different accounts, indicating three widely different attitudes about Jesus.

What happened when Jesus died?
John mentions nothing out of the ordinary and yet Luke and Mark say there was an eclipse with three hours of darkness in Mark and the veil in the temple being torn in two in Luke, something terrible for Jews. Matthew goes totally overboard. He mentions the veil but also speaks of an earthquake and the dead rising from their graves to walk through the streets, witnessed by many. Strange that the others fail to mention this incredible zombie event. It almost goes without saying that no non-biblical mention of it has been found.

Who witnessed the resurrection?
All four gospels vary between just Mary Magdalene or two Mary's and Salome and even Mary Magdalene, Joanna, Mary the mother of James, and the others. These may seem unimportant but keep in mind that, to Christians, this is the single most significant event in human history. Why are there any discrepancies at all?

When was the stone rolled away?
Three gospels state that the stone was already moved when Mary arrived but Matthew, ever one for drama, speaks of an earthquake and a real live angel rolling away the stone and sitting on it. Again, strange that something so incredible should be ignored by the other accounts.

What did the women do?
According to Matthew they ran to tell the disciples but Mark is clear that they told no-one. How can two 'gospels' be totally opposed?

What was the disciples' reaction?
Mark, usually our most reliable account, says nothing, whereas Luke has the disciples not believing and Luke and John have them seeking their own proof. Why so different?

When did the resurrected Jesus' first appear?
Matthew says he appeared to the women as they left the tomb but Luke says it was to two disciples (one named Cleopas) walking to Emmaus the same day. How can there be such major differences about something as earth shattering as Jesus' first rising from the dead?

Where was Jesus' second appearance?
In Matthew it was on a mountain in Galilee but Luke and John insist it was in Jerusalem. Which do we believe?

These discrepancies seem strange, especially as they are about some of the most amazing things to happen in the history of the world. Events vital to Christian belief. If we accept that the authors were not present and are merely reporting what they have heard, or perhaps the legends of their particular community based on oral tales, we may forgive them their differences but if, as we are told, the books are 'gospel' i.e. not only true but inspired by God and therefore totally reliable, we are left shaking our heads.

Returning briefly to deliberate changes, one glaring difference between later manuscripts and the earliest ones found is in the gospel of Mark. The early manuscripts of Mark end at 16.8. Three women go to Jesus' tomb but he is not there. A man tells them he has been resurrected and that they should tell the disciples to meet Jesus in Galilee but they run away, afraid and do not tell anyone. The end. Later scribes were clearly disturbed by such an abrupt ending and puzzled about how the disciples learned of Jesus' resurrection and where to meet him, so they added 12 verses. We know this because, in the original Greek, the writing style of that section is completely different and it clearly had a different author.

It is obvious then, that the gospels suffer from a number of problems:
A paucity of early manuscripts with which to authenticate the

stories.

This lack made worse by honest copying errors and deliberate changes.

Most importantly, the wildly varying accounts of some of the most significant events in human history.

The conclusion seems inescapable. We simply cannot know if the New Testament we read today is reliable or not. And if the stories of Jesus may not be accurate, how are we to know whether any of it is true? Jesus made it clear that his ministry was for the Jews alone and we already know that it was Saul/Paul who first preached to gentiles and really founded Christianity. And yet, millions of Christians today are blissfully unaware of these issues and still place absolute confidence in the Bible.

Should we tell them?

INTELLIGENT DESIGN.

REALLY?

Creationists who believe that their God (not anyone else's god) created the universe and everything in it, have a burden of proof which they cannot meet. The very idea of a deity that not only made everything but gets actively involved, is an extraordinary claim and, as Christopher Hitchens said

"Extraordinary claims require extraordinary evidence".

The problem for creationists is that no evidence exists.

As a way of examining this, let's take a look at what religious believers assert is God's most sublime creation, indeed the very reason for creating everything in the first place; the human body.

Far from being intelligently designed, the best you could say, if you were to accept the premise of a designer, is that she was incompetent.

What follows is a list of problems with the human body with a brief explanation of each. The information is not mine; it is taken directly from the Nautilus web site.

1. An unsound spine

Our spines are a mess. *"It's a wonder we can even walk"*, says Bruce Latimer, director of the Centre for Human Origins at Case Western Reserve University, Cleveland. When our ancestors walked on all fours, their spines arched, like a bow, to withstand the weight of the organs suspended below. But then we stood up. That threw the system out of whack by 90 degrees, and the spine was forced to become a column. Next, to allow for bipedalism, it curved forward at the lower back. And to keep the head in balance the upper spine curved in the opposite direction. This change put tremendous pressure on the lower vertebrae, giving lower back pain to about 80 percent of adults.

2. An inflexible knee

As Latimer says, "You take the most complex joint in the body and put it between two huge levers—the femur and the tibia— and you're looking for trouble". The upshot is that the knee only moves in two directions: forward and back. "That's why every major sport, except maybe rugby, makes it illegal to clip, or hit an opponent's knee from the side".

3. A pelvis too narrow

Childbirth hurts and, before modern surgery and medicine, it was often fatal. And to add insult to injury, the width of a woman's pelvis hasn't changed for some 200,000 years, keeping our brains from growing larger.

4. Exposed testicles

A man's life-giving organs hang vulnerably outside the body, in order to maintain a viable temperature for creating sperm.

5. Crowded teeth

Humans typically have three molars on each side of the upper and lower jaws, near the back of the mouth. When our brains drastically expanded in size, the jaw grew wider and shorter, leaving no room for the third, farthest back molars. These cusped grinders may have been useful before we learned to cook and process food, but now the 'wisdom teeth' are useless and mostly just get painfully impacted in the gums.

6. Meandering arteries

Blood flows into each of your arms and legs via one main artery, which enters the limb on the front side of the body, by the biceps or hip flexors. To supply blood to tissues at a limb's back side, such as the triceps and hamstrings, the artery branches out, taking circuitous routes around bones and bundling itself with nerves. This roundabout plumbing can make for some rather annoying glitches. At the elbow, for instance, an artery branch meets up with the ulnar nerve, which animates your little finger, just under the skin. That's why your arm goes numb when the lower tip of your upper arm bone, called the humerus or 'funny bone', takes a sharp blow.

7. A backward retina

"The photoreceptor cells in the retina of the eye are like microphones facing backward", explains Nathan Lents, an associate professor

of molecular biology at the City University of New York. This design forces light to travel the length of each cell, as well as through blood and tissue, to reach the equivalent of a receiver on the cell's backside. The setup may encourage the retina to detach from its supporting tissue—a leading cause of blindness. It also creates a blind spot where cell fibres, akin to microphone cables, converge at the optic nerve—making the brain refill the hole in the image.

8. A misrouted nerve

The recurrent laryngeal nerve (RLN) plays a vital role in our ability to speak and swallow. It feeds instructions from the brain to the muscles of the voice box, or larynx, below the vocal cords. Theoretically, the trip from brain to neck should be a quick one but during foetal development, the RLN gets entwined in a tiny lump of tissue in the neck, which descends to become blood vessels near the heart. That drop causes the nerve to loop around the aorta before traveling back up the larynx. Having this nerve in your chest makes it vulnerable during surgery—or a fist fight. The unnecessary journey is clear in humans but in Giraffes it is just crazy.

9. A misplaced voice box

The trachea (windpipe) and oesophagus (food pipe) open into the same space, the pharynx, which extends from the nose and mouth to the larynx (voice box). To keep food out of the trachea, a leaf-shaped flap called the epiglottis reflexively covers the opening to the larynx whenever you swallow. But sometimes, the epiglottis isn't fast enough. If you're talking and laughing while eating, food may slip down and get lodged in your airway, causing you to choke.

10. A klugey brain

"The human brain evolved in stages. As new additions were being built, older parts had to remain online to keep us up and running", explains psychologist Gary Marcus in his book, Kluge: The Haphazard Evolution of the Mind. And that live-in construction project led to slapdash workarounds. It's as if the brain were a dysfunctional workplace, where young employees (the forebrain) handle new-fangled technologies like language while the old guard (the midbrain and hindbrain) oversee the institutional memory—and the fuse box in the basement. This strange compartmentalisation has a few outcomes: depression, madness, unreliable memories, and confirmation bias.

That the above design flaws exist is not the issue. The question is; why would a perfect god make an imperfect creature. Every problem listed has a really easy solution, so why are they there?

All of the above flaws are explained by evolution. They occurred, for valid reasons, in non-human creatures and were retained when those creatures evolved. Evolutionary biologists have documented this process, both from other living animals and from the fossil record.
The intelligent design lobby denies evolution, but how are they to explain why their God made such obvious errors? Errors that have such easy solutions for a designer. If designers make a car and then notice it behaves in ways they did not foresee, a wobble on acceleration perhaps or poor braking, they simply change the design. If we can do it, why couldn't an all-powerful and omniscient god?

And just before I leave the subject, I would like, for a moment, to delve into the supposed intelligent design of the earth and the universe as a whole.
Religious believers would have us accept that not only did their particular god create everything, she did it with us in mind. Leaving aside the incredible solipsistic arrogance of that notion, it is interesting to ask a few simple questions.

Why, if such is the case, can humans only exist on a few limited areas of the earth? The majority of the earth is covered in water, in which we cannot survive without specialised man-made equipment. Even on land there are vast regions, such as deserts, active volcanoes and high mountains where humans cannot live without further man-made assistance. And that is on a planet supposedly made for us.

Why, if the universe was created to allow us to be placed on this planet, does it need to be such a terribly destructive environment? Why do millions of stars explode and die every day, taking with them all of their satellite planets and, possibly, destroying any life there may be?
Why does the universe need to be so unimaginably vast and why is it expanding with increasing velocity in every direction if it is there for us, as described in Genesis?

Far from being designed, let alone with us in mind, the universe is chaotic, dangerous and violent. The vast majority of it is utterly inimical to life of any kind, at least as we understand it. We must draw two possible conclusions. That either God is incompetent and wasteful on a cosmic scale or that God did not create the universe, or us.

SO, YOU'RE A CHRISTIAN?

For almost 1500 years there was only one western Christian tradition. At least, that is what we are taught. The only other form of Christianity was the eastern tradition, known today as the Orthodox Church, which we will discuss later. In reality, there were always different Christian sects and the church of Rome was just one of many. When it became predominant, by its association with the power of the Roman state, it began to seek out and eradicate the other forms of Christianity.

Then, in 1517, a German priest called Martin Luther decided that Roman Catholic church had become sickeningly corrupt and he nailed his 95 theses to the doors of his church. His intention was to highlight the issue and seek to clean up his beloved church but instead all hell broke loose.

Today, just over 500 years later, there are around 1000 different protestant sects and most of them actively dislike the others. How did this happen?

Part of the answer is obvious. Once you permit a division, there is nothing to prevent further division. But there is more to it than that.

We must give kudos to the early church for two things it did very well. The first thing we must grant is that it had determination and staying power. In the face of enmity and even direct persecution, it not only survived, it grew. The second thing we must grant is that it managed to align itself with the state apparatus of its harshest critic to become the state religion of Rome and in doing so it changed from persecuted to persecutor with an eagerness we should find disturbing. Whether this was down to clever strategy, luck or divine intervention is a matter of opinion but the results speak for themselves.

Once the Church was established as *the* Roman religion and all the other faiths and sects were driven out, it spread throughout the empire and even beyond, as those outside sought to emulate everything Roman and to integrate. It is true that some barbarian tribes adopted a different version of Christianity which was destined to cause even more sectarian bloodshed but Roman Christianity was now in charge. From that point on it had more than faith, it had very real secular power. It possessed the power of the state and, as the grip of that state slowly weakened, the church of Rome cleverly strengthened its grip on those who came next.

This power cannot be overstated. It ran from the right of Popes to crown kings, to the power to forbid ownership of the Bible to all but the clergy and to forbid Bibles in the vernacular. Both designed to ensure only the church's interpretation of scripture was promoted.
The church took money from kings and peasants alike and it demanded total obedience. It enforced its will on pain of eternal damnation and often, with the help of secular rulers, on pain of death.

At a time when virtually everyone in Europe was deeply religious, these threats were terrifyingly effective. It was a period when men looked to religion to explain everything and science as we know it did not exist. It was not until 1620 that Francis Bacon, the English philosopher statesman, published a work suggesting that experimentation and observation were better methods of seeking knowledge than simply reading ancient words and it was a hundred years after that before The Enlightenment saw individuals use science to explain the world and challenge the religious position.

As deeply corrupt as it undoubtedly was, the church protested against by a pious and deeply antisemitic Martin Luther was all powerful and all pervasive. Dissent was stamped out and contrary opinions persecuted, sometimes to the point of genocide. But it had already overreached.

By the time of Martin Luther, many were tired of church greed and its love of power. The relationship between Rome and the mostly German, Holy Roman Empire (neither holy nor Roman, nor even an empire, it adopted the name to add credibility and legitimacy) had been strained for many years, occasionally to breaking point and so the protests of a German priest fell on the ears of at least a few willing to listen. Those few included other learned men ready to establish a different kind of church, to worship God and follow the words of Jesus in a more simple and direct manner that did not involve earthly power and riches. The listeners included rulers too, who saw an opportunity to rid themselves of the grip of the Popes. So was born the European wars of religion that raged for hundreds of years and claimed the lives of millions, with all the combatants fighting in the name of the same God.

But something else was born too. The new protestant church was focussed on what it saw as correct forms of worship without corruption and so it made no attempt to create for itself a new hierarchy of power like that of Rome. Because of this, it was not long before further divisions showed themselves, often based upon the smallest of pretence. Indeed, today it is incredibly difficult for an outsider to recognise the differences between many of these Christian sects and the strong enmity between them seems comic.

The late Christopher Hitchens highlighted this in his biography of Thomas Jefferson. Jefferson wrote to the Baptists of Danbury, Connecticut, to assure them of the separation of church and state and his letter was in response to their request that something be done to protect them from persecution. And who were the persecutors? The Congregationalists of Danbury, who had control of the local government at the time. The really crazy part, at least to those whose thinking is not clouded by faith, is that Baptists *are* congregationalist, in that they do not believe in any form of hierarchy and the differences between the two Christian groups are ridiculously small. But not so small that one could not oppress the other to the point where the Baptists wrote to the President of the United States for help.

All this leads, finally and somewhat tortuously, to my point. If you are a Christian, which type of Christian are you? Moreover, why aren't you a different type?

The answer to both of these is usually that you were raised that way by parents and community. In other words, you did not have a choice. By the time you were old enough to think for yourself, you were thoroughly inculcated. I am told that indoctrinated is a word too strong to use.

But if that is the case, how do you know that your way is indeed the right way? Do you even know what differentiates your church from the others? More importantly, why would an all-knowing, all-powerful God allow people to worship him in different ways? He supposedly gave us free will, but why would he allow that free will to make such a fundamental error when to correct it would be as easy as a quick personal appearance, a clearer set of instructions in a holy book or perhaps a few revelations? After all, once he had cleared up the issue of how to worship, he could leave us to carry on as before but with even greater certainty of his love and power.

The answer, of course, is that these tiny differences aren't really important to God, but then why would men maintain the myriad of different sects? Why not simply accept that it has all been a mistake and unite into a single, protestant, church?
Because the differences and the prejudice they create have absolutely nothing to do with God and everything to do with human nature. So, how can they be justified in terms of God's worship?

But, to go back a step, now that the Catholic church no longer practices the forms of corruption highlighted by Martin Luther, (at least not as obviously) why not re-unite into a single Christianity? Because many more differences have arisen since the 1500's and too much blood has been spilt. Protestants and Catholics are diametrically opposed and in many cases are extremely violent towards one another. And all in the name of the same God, who simply allows it to happen.

Christians explain all the horrors of the world by citing two excuses. The first is that God promised not to intervene again, after he virtually wiped out all life on earth in a temper tantrum. The second is that God gave us free will and whatever we do is our own fault.

These excuses are simply not convincing. Non-believers see them as a cop out. The non-interference promise was ignored by God, as may be seen in Numbers 16, where the people of the Exodus complain about the sole leadership of Moses and Aaron and the two men ask God to intervene. God, in his usual way, doesn't send a sign to support his favourites, nor does he change the hearts of the others, he kills all the dissenters. God then goes full genocidal and sends a plague to wipe out his own chosen people. Aaron manages to stop the plague with some incense but not before thousands died, by God's hand.

God is often referred to as our father but what kind of parent allows his children to play in areas he knows to be dangerous and sits back when those dangers hurt or kill his children?

What kind of parent allows his children so much freedom that they fight and injure themselves, even to the point where one child kills another, while he simply watches?

What kind of parent loses his temper so badly that he must be stopped from murdering his own children?

The answer to this thorny problem is usually that 'God works in mysterious ways' or 'it is not given to us to understand the mind of God', or better yet, 'God has a plan'.

Again, not convinced.

Ultimately, most Christians do not wrestle with such issues. Most Christians follow what I call the Sunday School approach to religion. Their understanding of the Bible and of their faith is no more sophisticated than what they learned as a child, backed up by some pleasant tales spun by preachers. And that's OK. Their faith is a comfort and I understand that. But being a comfort does not make it true.

If you are a Christian, should you not seek to understand everything about Christianity? Everything about its history, its beliefs and its teachings? When you begin a new job, you try to learn everything about it. When you begin a new relationship, you wish to know the other person completely. How much more important is your religion? How much more important is the thing which governs your entire life?

The strangest thing about religion is that it works best in ignorance. The more you know, the harder it is to believe.

So, you're a Christian? But what do you truly know about Christ, about the religion and about your sect? Please try the challenges below. It might reinforce your faith but it will, at the very least, help you to learn about something which is, supposedly, the most important thing in your life.

Really learn about Christ. Read your Bible, Old and New Testament, with a detailed and critical eye.
Notice all the contradictions and the obvious nonsense.
Learn about the history of Christianity and the horrors perpetrated in its name.
Learn about the way many of the things you think you know were taken from other, pre-existing, religions.
Learn about the details and the history of what your sect believes and, more importantly, why.
If you believe in the Trinity, learn how the earlier Bible manuscripts, written in Greek have no mention of it and how it was added later in Latin translations.

Then come back and tell me if you still believe.

OLD TESTAMENT FAILS

And the consequence of believing them

All Jews are expected to believe in the Tanakh; a collection of books that Christians call the Old Testament, beginning with the Torah, the five 'Books of Moses', or the Pentateuch. Christians, despite believing that Jesus is more important than the old stories, still include the Old Testament in their Bible and Muslims acknowledge that much of the Quran includes versions of Bible stories. But is it reliable? Is it fact or only myth?

In form, most of the Old Testament reads as a history of the Hebrews as they became the Israelites and the Jews. It reaches from the creation of the world, through God choosing them as his people, the sojourn in Egypt, the exodus, their many trials and tribulations including the captivity in Babylon and the return. There is then a 400 year gap before the events described in the New Testament of the Christians.

To discover whether the Old Testament is anything more than myths and legends, masquerading as a creation story and history, I will analyse a number of prominent sections from the book of Genesis, the first book of the Old Testament and touching upon the Exodus story in the eponymously named second book. These sections cover the creation of the Earth and the important early events in what is supposed to be the history of the world in general and the Hebrew people in particular.
It is important to recognise that showing these books to be factually incorrect does not mean the rest of the Bible is also false but it does cast doubt. The story of King David may be analysed in isolation and compared with what we know from archaeology to ascertain its reliability but, as it forms part of the same work as the areas we will study here, it is enough to say that we should begin any such analysis with scepticism.

Who wrote the five books of Moses? Tradition says Moses himself was the author but this is clearly wrong. There are different writing styles, all references to Moses are written in the third person and the books end with an account of his death and the events immediately after his demise. Also, Moses is referred to as "the most humble man who ever lived"; not really something a humble man would say about himself. An additional clue that Genesis at least was not written by Moses may be found in G14, which refers to the town of Dan. The book of Judges, covering a far later period, states the town was called Laish and wasn't renamed until over 300 years after Moses' death. Our first clue that the Bible is unreliable, as both contradictory claims cannot be true.

In reality, millions of people today still follow and believe, or at the very least are inspired by, a collection of books written in the bronze age, when people knew little about the world, let alone the wider universe. Books which presumably codified older oral traditions and are full of things for which there is no evidence whatsoever and things that we now know to be impossible. Books written by unknown authors that contradict themselves and were written hundreds of years after the events mentioned. If that seems a harsh assessment, what follows are just a few examples.

Genesis. The Creation myth.
The first book of the Bible explains, in detail, how the world was created by God. Clearly the author wasn't there to witness it, so we are expected to believe that God provided the author with such knowledge sometime later. The problem is that there are two different versions of the creation mashed together in one book. These presumably represent two differing oral traditions because they can't both be true. But if the story is narrated or inspired by God, why would God get the story wrong or allow mistakes to enter his holy book?

A few specifics which prove the creation myth to be nonsense.
God said let there be light.
But he had yet to create the sun and we now know that there is no light without it.
God separated night from day.
Without the Sun and the rotation of a globe-like earth, this is not

possible.

God created a dome in the waters that covered the earth and he called the dome the sky. This separated the waters above from the waters below.

We now know the world is not flat with a sky dome over it and there are no waters above.

In G1.11. God creates all vegetation, plants and fruit trees.

But he had yet to create the Sun to provide energy through photosynthesis so they would all die. Also, without the Sun, the Earth would be a lifeless frozen ball of ice-covered rock. In reality, the earth had no oxygen to support plant life for at least 2 billion years and the oxidation took place slowly, through photosynthesis, beginning with single celled life in the oceans.

God created lights in the dome of Sky to mark out seasons, days and years.

We now know that stars are not placed in a sky dome simply for us to know the seasons. This knowledge is part of understanding that we are not the centre of a creation with us in mind.

On the fourth day God finally gets around to creating the Sun and the Moon.

This idea of the Earth first was plausible to ancient minds but, because we have witnessed it occurring elsewhere, we now be fairly sure that our solar system formed around 4.5 billion years ago from a dense cloud of interstellar gas and dust. The cloud collapsed, possibly due to the shockwave of a nearby exploding star, forming a solar nebula—a spinning, swirling disk of material. Gravity pulled more and more material in, until the pressure in the core was so great that hydrogen atoms began fuse into helium, releasing a tremendous amount of energy. With that, our Sun was born, and it eventually amassed more than 99 percent of the available matter. Matter farther out in the disk was also clumping together, smashing into one another, forming larger and larger objects, some of them big enough for their gravity to shape them into spheres, becoming planets, dwarf planets and large moons.

G1.22 -25. God creates all living things.

G1.27. God creates humankind, men and women, in his image but no mention of a single couple.

All this took 6 days and he rested on the seventh.

But……. And this is where it gets interesting,

G2.5 -7. God creates Adam before there was any other living thing on earth.

The opposite of the earlier version.

G2.8. First mention of the Garden.

G2.19. God creates all animals and birds and brings them to Adam to be named.

With millions of species, that must have taken some time. It is also the opposite way round to the earlier version, where the living things are created before man.

G2.22 God creates woman from Adam's rib.

Created separately and in a different way from the earlier version.

Forbidden fruit

In Genesis 3 we reach the serpent and the forbidden fruit story, in which God deliberately puts a tree in the garden, from which Adam and Eve are not supposed to eat. So why put it there at all? God then lies about the consequences of eating the fruit and it's the serpent that tells the truth. God punishes Adam and Eve, for using the free will he gave them and for giving in to the temptation that he deliberately put in their way. This seems a little unfair. He also punishes the serpent, for telling the truth.

But God doesn't just punish Adam and Eve, he punishes every human that will ever live. And it gets worse.

According to Christian tradition, Adam & Eve's 'original sin' of eating a forbidden fruit, was so terrible that it divided all men from God and God later had to sacrifice his son (who is also himself) to himself in order to forgive all mankind for their part in that sin and be reconciled with him. This doesn't even seem sane, let alone believable. What kind of tyrant deliberately creates a situation, knowing the result and then punishes not only the individual whom he deliberately manipulated into doing wrong but every human being from that time onward?

In G3.22. God speaks. "See, the man has become like one of us, knowing good and evil; and now, he might reach out his hand and take also from the tree of life, and eat, and live forever". Firstly, who is the 'us', God refers to? It has been suggested that this is something akin to the royal 'we' used by British monarchy and still only refers to God alone but this misunderstands the expression. In fact, it was Henry II who first employed it in referring to himself and God as being of one mind. In Genesis, God's use of the phrase 'one of us' clearly demonstrates that there were other gods. Secondly, if Adam and Eve could become immortal gods simply by eating from two fruit trees, why put the trees in the garden when they could have been planted anywhere in God's creation? This demonstrates a very human, localised way of thinking.

The first people
Adam and Eve had two sons, Cain and Able. Along with Mom & Dad, they were the only people on earth. So, who did the sons marry? God must have made more people for the boys to marry, although the Bible is strangely silent about such an incredible thing. God must also have made a lot more people, to live in the cities the boys built, presumably on their own, but again the Bible is silent about all these new people.

We then get the names of the generations of offspring and their individual lifespans of many hundreds of years. Methuselah was 969 years old when he, eventually, died. Most Christians remain quiet about this, in case we might think it's all nonsense.

Noah and the flood
A whole book could be written about how nonsensical this story really is, but here are just a few points, taken from a previous

article.

- An impossibly old man builds a boat which, by the dimensions in the text, could not have been big enough.
- In just one week, he gathered together representatives of every animal on earth.
- Billions of cubic miles of water appeared, from places that simply do not exist.
- The whole world was covered with water 5.5 miles deeper than the initial sea level, in order to
cover the mountains.
- God sent a wind and the water went back to the non-existent places from whence it came.
- After what must have been an indescribably horrible 7.5 months, spent feeding and cleaning up after the representatives of up to 8.5 million species, they came out into a cleansed world.
- Animals and men somehow managed to find food in this cleansed and drowned world and to spread to every corner of the globe. The herbivores were presumably delighted to find their food still lived, after spending months under 5 miles of water and the carnivores must have been happy to go vegetarian for a few years, until the herbivores had expanded to a population size that could withstand predation.
- The humans divided into races as diverse as Eskimos and Pygmies, Chinese, Europeans and Zulus.
- This happened really quickly, because the Bible makes it clear that within the period of its writing, the
- middle east was occupied by Egyptians, Assyrians, Babylonians, Philistines etc. Remembering of course that the authors had no knowledge of the world beyond and so could not mention other races.

The final part of the story is also problematic and usually not discussed. Noah gets drunk and lies naked in his tent. His son Ham sees this, tells his brothers and the other two cover up their father without looking. For the terrible crime of accidently walking in on his drunken naked father, Noah curses Ham. But, he doesn't actually curse his son. Oh no. Taking his example from God's tendency to overreact, he actually curses his grandson and every subsequent generation to be slaves to the offspring of the other two sons. Forever. I've heard of abusive fathers but this clearly this makes no sense. However, it might just reflect the morals and culture of the person who wrote the fairy story, as well as justifying why it was fine to take slaves from other tribes.

Other places and people

After the Noah story we get an account of the generations that follow and how they gave rise to the nations and people of various countries. It is significant that only the lands of the Middle East are mentioned. The author clearly had no knowledge of the rest of the world. Which begs the question, where did all the other people come from? As a brief aside here, it is worth looking at a map of the world and drawing a circle which encompasses all the events of the Bible. The circle is very small indeed.

A big tower

All the people of the earth, from Eskimos to Kalahari Bushmen, supposedly spoke the same language. They decided to build a tower to the heavens to make a name for themselves. Question: If it was the decision of all men, who were they trying to impress? Apart from the fact that an understanding of physics reveals that mud bricks do not have the necessary compression strength to support a structure that threatened to reach the heavens, the story also presupposes that people with differing languages would not be capable of advancing mankind's knowledge and that God would be threatened by such knowledge. We now know that people with different languages can work perfectly well together and accomplish great things. It is also firmly against the idea of an omniscient, omnipotent God to think that mankind's advancement would be threatening. It is true that increasing knowledge threatens religious belief but, of course, that is completely different.

Abraham and a Lot more (sorry)
The story now moves forward, hundreds of years, to tell of Abram and God's promise to an old man that he would have children that would become a nation.

The story speaks of Abram and his wife, Sarai, going to Egypt. In order to ensure Abram gets all the goods he wants, Abram pretends Sarai is his sister and the Pharaoh then marries Sarai. God then punishes the Pharaoh and his family with great plagues, even though the Pharaoh has done no wrong and was lied to and tricked by Abram and his wife, who get away without God's punishment.

When Abram was one hundred years old and Sarai ninety, God promised to make Abram 'exceedingly fertile' and Sarai had a son called Isaac. Abram would become Abraham, Sarai was to be Sarah and Isaac would be the father of a great nation. From then on, all men had to be circumcised, because apparently genital mutilation is the way to signify a deal with God. Thus began three thousand years of the unnecessary butchery of male children, which later gave rise to an even worse barbaric practice against the female children of Muslims and others.

Abraham's nephew, Lot, was living in the city of Sodom and God decided that Sodom and Gomorrah were so full of evil that they must be destroyed. Lot negotiated with God that the people would be spared if 10 good people could be found. Two angels came to Sodom to check it out and Lot took them in but the men of the town wanted to rape them. Lot then offered his virgin daughters to be raped instead. The men attacked Lot but the Angels pulled him inside the house and struck the men blind so they could not find Lot's door, but the men kept attacking, which showed real commitment. I'm not sure I would be able to hold on to my lustful thoughts in the face of sudden blindness. Leaving aside the economic consequences for a town that had a reputation for the homosexual rape of strangers, it is unclear how offering your virgin daughters instead is a good thing.

In order to destroy the cities, God rains sulphur, in the first occurrence of chemical warfare in history. Lot and his family escape the town but his wife turns back to look and is turned into salt. This whole story is full of strangeness. It suggests that Lot offering his daughters to be gang raped was a good thing. It suggests that angels who can strike men blind needed Lot's help. It suggests that gay lust is not diminished by being struck blind and it suggests that seeing a city destroyed by fire and sulphur would somehow turn someone to salt.
Do you recall the little discussed end to Noah's tale? Well here again there is something which is often left out. After the dust had settled, Lot's daughters get him drunk, sleep with him and become pregnant. There is no suggestion of punishment for this incest and, by this stage in the tale, it almost seems normal.

In G20.2, Abraham tries the same lie about his wife being his sister, this time to King Abimelech of Gerar. He was clearly not the most moral of people to choose as founder of a people. This time though, God warns the King and disaster is averted, but the book says nothing about God having a quiet word with Abraham about his repeated bad behaviour. We also learn that Sarah was Abraham's half-sister. With the early populating of the earth, Lot's daughters and now Abraham being married to his sister, it seems incest wasn't as uncommon as it is today and God clearly approved. It should also be noted that by this time *Abraham and Sarah were old and well stricken in age; and it ceased to be with Sarah after the manner of women*". We might wonder about a king who is so easily fooled by a couple of old folks that it needed God to have a word in his ear.

A sacrifice
We finally come to the part where God instructs Abraham to

sacrifice his son, Isaac. The story is questionable for the following reason. If God is truly omniscient, he must know what is in a man's heart and if that is the case, why test Abraham's faith unnecessarily with such a cruel demand? If God needs to test Abraham, he is not omniscient and therefore not worthy of worship. If God was merely using a mean trick, he is immoral and not worthy of worship.

The exodus

We will now skip forward over 400 years, to the story of the exodus. We will pass over the tale of the Israelites in Egypt (pun very much intended), ignore the magic trick contest between Moses and the Pharaoh's advisors and we will even ignore the plagues, pausing only to ponder on the story that God hardened Pharaoh's heart and caused him to deny the Israelites, thereby deliberately causing the plagues, the suffering and the deaths of the pursuing Egyptian army. It seems an unnecessary and awful thing for God to do. Why not just soften the Pharaoh's heart instead and make him let the Israelites leave without all the fuss?

When the Israelites were finally allowed to leave Egypt, the Bible says there were 600,000 men, along with all the women and children and large herds of livestock. Estimates of the total number of people vary but it must have been well over a million.

Ancient Egypt was roughly the same size as the modern country and its population at that has been estimated to around 3 million. Imagine for a moment a society of 3 million that holds one million people in bondage, suddenly letting them go. Imagine the devastating social and economic consequences. Now imagine the logistics of gathering a million people together in a single group and guiding them around a desert, for 40 years. How many tens of thousands would die in that time? How much of an effect would such a prolonged mass migration, going around in circles in a relatively small area, have on the land? And yet there is no evidence that any of the story ever happened.

The Egyptians were obsessed with writing and record keeping and, because the dry desert is nearly perfect for preserving everything from stone carvings to paper documents, we have literally millions of artefacts, scrolls, writing tablets and stone carved hieroglyphs. And yet there is absolutely no evidence of the exodus tale whatsoever. Nothing.

No records of the Israelites in Egypt for over 400 years. No carvings, no writings, no bones with Jewish DNA, no records by the Egyptians.   It has been suggested that the Egyptians erased all records, but they tried and failed to remove all traces of one pharaoh, because he tried to introduce belief in a single god. In another example, Pharoah Tuthmosis, tried to remove all references of his mother and co-ruler and failed. How then did they manage to wipe out all mention of the existence of the Israelites in their midst for over 4 centuries, the plagues and the deaths of all the firstborn and the mass exodus of a million people and the problems it must have caused?

In an area so dry that we can find the remains of a single campfire a thousand years old, Israeli archaeologists working for many years, intent on finding proof of the Bible stories, found absolutely nothing to suggest a million people spent forty years wandering an area the size of West Virginia.

Finally and conclusively, during the time that the Bible says the exodus happened, the area of the 'promised land' was ruled by Egypt. Fleeing Egyptian tyranny and spending almost two generations in the desert in order to move to a place ruled by your oppressors makes no sense. It is even less likely that after the Israelite slaves escaped with the help of God wiping out the army, the Egyptians would stand by as genocide was committed against their client kingdoms, with a subsequent reduction of revenue and a loss of the military buffer zone between Egypt and other powerful enemies.

What happened when the vast horde of people were finally

allowed to reach the promised land? Did they scatter and find places to farm and live as one peaceful community, safe in a land promised to them by God? No. Because there were already a great many people living there. This land promised to them and sold by God as being wonderful wasn't even theirs. At the border, they were told by God to attack the inhabitants. The Bible doesn't record whether any of them wondered about obeying a god who had clearly misled them. And then things really take a turn towards the dark side. Not content with simply beating or driving out the original inhabitants, God commands that his chosen people must commit genocide. They must kill every man, woman, child and even the animals. But it was OK to leave young virgin girls alive. I wonder why.

The Bible is filled with similar problems but I feel the point is made. The Tanakh or Old Testament simply cannot be relied upon as either history or holy book. It tells some wonderful stories, along with a great deal of horror and behaviour which would be unspeakably wrong today, committed by men on God's orders and directly by God. It also sheds light on what an ancient people believed about themselves. But it is nothing more than myth and legend. A fancied and fantastic oral creation myth, for a people almost continually oppressed, that explained their problems as God's punishment for their wrongdoing and offered hope of better times.

The people that made up these stories lived in a time where mankind knew little of their world and absolutely nothing of the solar system and the universe. The whole span occurs within a very small area of the earth but, to the authors, it felt like the whole world. The events described simply cannot have happened.

In one incident not related above, God makes the Sun stand still, to allow time for his chosen people to kill more enemies. This may have seemed plausible to people who believed not only in an all-powerful God but that the Sun was a light, placed in the sky by that God. But for it to actually happen, the Earth would need to stop spinning; to go from over 1000 miles an hour to zero in an instant. If that occurred, the atmosphere would still be in motion, meaning rocks, topsoil, trees, buildings, people and animals would be swept away at an incredible and devastating speed. People might notice. But then Egypt and other places on earth had thriving civilisations at the time of Noah's flood and they seem not to have noticed the 5 miles of water on top of them.

All of this, of course, begs a question. Why do people still believe in the Bible?

The truth is that most Jews and Christians do not read the Bible and many never have. They know a few of the stories, as told to them as children or by their preachers or read out during prayer services, but they spend little or no time actually thinking about their holy book or the claims made by their faith.

There is, of course, another much smaller group. Fundamentalists, who claim every word of the holy book is true and that the Bible is a factual and very real account of creation and history. In order to do so, they deny the claims of science and seek to force our increasing knowledge of the universe into something which fits their pre-formed and unalterable picture. They claim that God really did create the earth in six days, as described in Genesis and that God really did make the Sun stand still. That these things are true because God used miracles to make it so.

Such views were once common. More than four hundred years ago, when there were no better sources of information, it was perfectly natural and excusable for people to accept the Bible as literal truth, although even then there were sceptics. In fact, there have always been those who questioned, but before the Reformation exposed the staggering levels of corruption in the church and the Enlightenment provided new ways of reasoning, the church held sufficient power to suppress, persecute and kill anyone who openly spoke of their doubts. And when movements sprang up to express a Christianity different to the dogma, its followers were pursued and massacred.

In the modern world, to claim that the Bible is without error, let alone correct in its description of the creation, is not about doubting that science has all the answers, nor is it about the idea that faith and science play different roles. It is to deliberately refuse to see the world as it is.

It is important to understand that this is not about belief in God; it is perfectly possible to believe in a deity, without the need to take the Bible literally. Claiming the Bible is literally true is a conscious decision to reject all of mankind's scientific and technological advances of the past four centuries and more. To believe otherwise is not logical. So much of what we take for granted in the modern world simply would not work if the earth was flat, under a sky dome and if the celestial bodies were placed in the dome by God in order to assist mankind.

Sadly, it is impossible to reach such closed minds and all debate with them is a waste of effort. How can one conduct a meaningful dialogue with someone who refuses to listen because they are convinced you are a sinner, or under the influence of the devil, if you do not fully accept all of the outrageous nonsense they espouse? Nonetheless, we must continue to strive against this ridiculous worldview and to educate the more moderate believers who are unaware of the inescapable conclusions drawn by their beliefs.

Finally, I want to highlight the inevitable end-result of allowing such thinking to thrive.

Whilst any adult must be free to believe whatever they choose; we must all be vigilant and work unceasingly to ensure such nonsense does not infect our children. Bad ideas are like a poison for the mind; they do not remain isolated but spread

to infect our thinking in other areas. Allowing our children to believe the ridiculous notion that the Bible is truth would prevent all future scientific discovery and advancement and drag us back to a time where religion held power over everyone and heresy was punishable with death.
The word 'heresy', incidentally, originally meant making choices, something that religions simply will not allow.

I hope you will forgive me as, for my conclusion, I divert on to a tangent, but one not too far from my main topic.

Whilst the majority of Christians and Christian churches around the world now accept evolution as fact, there is a marked reluctance to do so in the United States of America. And it is not only evangelical preachers and apologists who deny evolution. There is a widespread belief, among up to 50% of the population that evolutionary scientists are mistaken, at best, or colluding in some weird conspiracy, at worst. Although why thousands of scientists all around the word would be a part of such a conspiracy and what their purpose might be is not clear.
But does such ignorance really matter?

Claiming that evolution is wrong, merely demonstrates a lack of understanding and an unwillingness to look at the evidence, coupled with a refusal to admit that the preachers of one's church probably don't know as much about the subject as biologists and may be in error. But to insist that creationism be taught in schools with equal validity, or even in place of evolution, is to teach children that scientific and critical thinking are incorrect and unimportant. It teaches that religious explanations are more valid, more important and more trustworthy than scientific ones. Once that principal is established in the minds of children, there is no way to teach them what they need to know in order to succeed as adults in the modern world.

If we allow this to continue and to grow, within two generations our children will be fit only to follow like sheep, hold manual or menial jobs and to mistrust anyone brighter or better educated. We will have returned to the bronze age. That future looks dark indeed.

A CHOSEN PEOPLE

Almost everyone in the western world and the middle east, are familiar with the biblical idea of the Jews being God's chosen people. Jewish people today still believe it, albeit that, in light of their past and present troubles, many follow the statement with a semi-humorous question, "Chosen for what?". But Christians are taught that Jesus signified the end of the old covenant between God and the Jews and the establishment of a new one making Christians the new chosen people.

The big problem with the whole notion of a chosen people is that it is elitist. It automatically excludes everyone else. If you are chosen to be God's favourite and your place in heaven is reserved, everybody else is going to the other place, or have to work harder to have a chance at their golden ticket. That is a deeply unpleasant philosophy. Throughout our history, whenever one group of humans sought to oppress another, they began by disseminating the idea that the others were inferior and that whatever was done to them did not matter.

Christians like to think of themselves as peaceful, loving people, following the teachings of Jesus meek and mild and the God of love. They are either unaware of the bloody history of Christianity, or choose to ignore it, just as they tend to ignore the fundamentalists within their ranks. At the same time, they characterise Muslims by the actions of a tiny minority who commit acts of violence and this reinforces their sense of superiority. The strange thing is that whilst Christians think themselves superior, Muslims are equally convinced that they are God's chosen and the Jews deny that their original agreement with God ever ended.

Clearly, they can't all be right. But, as has been noted before, they can all be wrong. Under analysis, we see that there is absolutely no evidence that any such covenant with God exists, for any religion, except words in books. And, despite the claims that they are all sent by God, the books are not mutually compatible.

To believe you are chosen, it is necessary to believe a number of other things.

First, that your God exists.

This may seem obvious but this simple first step excludes all other gods and their worshippers.

Second, that your specific way of worshipping 'the' God, is the correct one and all others are wrong.

You have no evidence for this view, only biased belief.

Third, that God is likely to have a favourite, to the exclusion of the rest of mankind.

Again, this simple belief entails more assumptions than many people realise. It assumes the creator of mankind plays favourites and is comfortable with selecting one group, to the exclusion of the rest of humanity who are after all a part of his creation. This selection would be based solely upon the acceptance of a revelation only offered to a tiny number of people in a poor backwater and that although the message was not given to other people, they were nonetheless expected to learn it, and believe it completely, by human transmission alone. Moreover, it presumes that an omniscient God would create mankind, knowing from the beginning that the majority of them would not make the cut. For Christians it is necessary to believe that God *always* knew the Jews would not accept Jesus, *always* knew Jesus would need to be killed and *always* knew that his covenant with the Jews would then be broken. This gives rise to many other questions about the infallibility and the character of God.

Of course, most Christians, or other religious believers, never consider the above issues. To them, the idea of being chosen is only a good thing. They do not lie awake at night thinking of the darker implications. Thinking of the fate of billions of people, throughout history and today, who are not chosen. But that darker side is a very real result of the elitist idea. We can be thankful then, that the notion of being chosen is simply man-made nonsense.

To some extent, all religious believers think they are the chosen, because they all think their god is the only real one, or their way of worshiping the God is the only valid one. Just like everyone thinks their country or their football team is the best and every child thinks their Dad is the toughest and/or smartest. The pattern is clear.

Ultimately, of course, such beliefs are neither logical nor rational, but they are understandable, as nothing more than a perfectly natural personal bias. With the exception of conversions, religious belief is an accident of birth. If you are born in the United States, you are probably going to be Christian. If you are born in Saudi Arabia, you are probably going to be Muslim, if you are born in India, you are probably going to be Hindu. Once you are born and raised in a particular religion, you are likely to accept the tenets of that religion, including its ideas of superiority and truth, in contrast to other, clearly misguided, beliefs. You do not accept them because you have thought carefully and made an informed decision but because they were taught to you, with authority, as a child. You then care little about other beliefs and do nothing to educate yourself about them. This lack of interest information about the alternatives creates cognitive bias and actively prevents dissent.

What this demonstrates is that what you believe has absolutely nothing to do with any inherent truth but is merely a result of where and when you were born and what your family and community believe. Regardless of what those things might be. However improbable and implausible are the stories of your holy books, you will believe them, just as you scorn the stories of other faiths that are, from the outside, no more or less unlikely than yours. To Christians, the story of Mohammed flying to Jerusalem on a winged horse is laughable but they have no problem believing that God spoke to Moses through a burning bush, or that Jesus cast demons into pigs. Viewed from the outside, none of these stories is more or less likely to be true than the others.

Thankfully, we have now created virtually unlimited access to information and whilst we may not be getting smarter, it is at least possible to be better informed. Over the last three hundred years, since the Enlightenment, we have become aware of alternatives to religious thought. Where humans once filtered all knowledge and all experience through their religious beliefs, we now look to science. And science is not simply a different way of interpreting the world, it is an entirely different way of thinking. Whilst religions discourage questions and exhort people to simply believe, to the point where faith itself is seen as a virtue, science involves the testing of hypothesis and the search for facts, provable through empirical evidence, rather than for truths declared as such through pre-existing belief.

Where religions once held the power to hold back human progress, by declaring that nothing worthwhile may found outside of the holy books, we are now free to ask questions, to discover amazing wonders and to create technology based upon scientific facts.

We have come far but we have much further to travel. We are still shackled by ideas that were born in the childhood of our species. Books written in the bronze age, by people who knew little of the world outside of their immediate neighbourhood and absolutely nothing of the wider universe beyond the sky. Books and letters written by people who already believed in the divinity of someone they had never met and who wrote from faith, not fact. Or a book written by a desert dwelling trader and warlord fourteen hundred years ago who preached love & acceptance and hatred & warfare in equal measure, leaving people unsure and with so many ways of interpreting his words that they have sought to destroy each other ever since.
And, lest we become complacent in our knowledge of the world, we should keep in mind that Islam once represented

the pinnacle of scientific endeavour in many fields and that, for a number of reasons, that impetus was lost. Today, sadly, many Muslims seem more interested in living like their prophet did, fourteen hundred years ago, than in pursuing knowledge through science.

We will, eventually, outgrow such childish ideas as race and religious belief. Ideas that still cause us to hate and kill our fellow men over tiny differences, whilst choosing to ignore the vast array of things that make us the same. We will come to understand that there is no one race or group which is superior to another through divine fiat. We will come to realise that to be elitist always entails relegating others to a position of unimportance and that allows us to act in ways which have appalling consequences.

There is no chosen people, just as there is no true religion. Both are man-made ideas. If you doubt this and hold to a belief in your god and your superiority, ask yourself a question. Is it likely that your all-knowing, all-loving god would create humanity, in the knowledge that in the future he would be saving only a tiny number of them and condemning the rest to eternal torture? Does that not seem a cruel and wasteful thing to do? Does that god not seem capricious, heartless and therefore unworthy of your devotion? If you believe your god to be the only one, the creator, the father, you must also believe him to be omniscient, omnipresent and all-powerful. If that is so, why would such a god want an ignorant people committed to killing and oppressing their fellows in his name?

Islam. Miracle or Fabrication?

Like all religions, Islam has a story, an account of how and why the religion came to be. For Muslims, of course, the story is wonderful, in the original sense of the word and filled with improbable but true events that are all the more wonderful *because* they are improbable. The notion that they are improbable because they did not happen is not considered, indeed cannot be considered as to do so is to commit the gravest of sins.

Whilst many of the world's religions are ancient, with their stories shrouded by the mists of time, Islam had its beginning when written history already existed. Although it happened around 1400 years ago, the events coincide with people, places and other non-Islamic events that we know from history to be genuine. It is therefore easy to simply accept that the story of the birth of Islam is true, even if non-believers might question some of the more incredible details, such as the prophet Mohammed flying on a horse. But what if none of it were true?

My purpose here is *not* to state that Islam is a lie, nor will I claim that Allah does not exist, or Mohammed was not his prophet or the events surrounding the birth of Islam did not take place. I have no evidence to support such assertions and to do so would be foolish and misleading. I merely propose that the incredible elements of the story should be examined without the prejudice of faith. Whilst I understand fully that to Muslims, even the idea of this procedure is insulting, that cannot be helped. What follows will be done calmly and considerately and if Islam and individual Muslims are unwilling or unable to stand firm in the light of examination, I suggest the problem lies there.

The story begins in Mecca, a trading town deep in the Arabian desert. The town belongs to the Quraishi, one of many Arabian tribes who, when not trading across vast distances, made war upon each other and against larger neighbouring nations. The eastern Roman empire, also known as the Byzantines from their capital, later to be called Constantinople and today, Istanbul, had a long-standing conflict with the region's other superpower, the Sassanid dynasty of the Persians and instead of using up their own manpower, both sides made use of Arab tribes as mercenaries in proxy fights.

Although pagans themselves, the Arabs were trapped between the Zoroastrian Persians and the Christian Romans, with Jewish settlements and traders in the mix. They could not have avoided some knowledge of these religions nor it is likely their influence. This was the situation when, according to the Islamic story, in 610AD, a forty-year-old illiterate trader named Mohammed was visited by the angel Gabriel.

The angel commanded that Mohammed read what he would provide. There is a dispute in Islam over Mohammed's reaction but the Sunni majority believe that Mohammed said he could not read and the angel ignored this plea three times and pressed a hand to Mohammed's chest and miraculously, the man was able to read and remember the three passages given. Shia Muslims believe that far from being surprised by Gabriel, Mohammed already knew his life's purpose and was familiar with the angel. They further say that there was no need for the angel to pressure Mohammed either verbally or physically. A parallel may be drawn here between the differences in the Christian Bible between the synoptic gospels, who portray Jesus as a man who struggles with his role as redeemer and the gospel of John, which has Jesus as divine, powerful and resolved and needing no help from any man. Whether we are considering the two descriptions of Jesus or the two of Mohammed, both versions cannot be true.

Whichever version of events is believed, what happened next is of more importance. Over a period of time, the angel recited more and more passages to Mohammed until the whole of the Quran was complete in the man's mind. But he did not write it down. Mohammed spread the word that a new way to save mankind had been revealed to him and people began to believe and follow him. This did not sit well with the leaders of the tribe and Mohammed and his followers had to flee to the town of Yathrib, later called Medina, where he gathered his strength. He and his followers raided the Quraishi and things became tense. Mohammed was victorious and so began the spread of Islam, throughout the Arabian Peninsula and its tribes. Mohammed died before the campaign could be pressed into other lands but his successors, the Caliphs, continued the work.

Islamic apologists get irate when it is suggested that Islam was spread by the sword and they dispute the notion that the conquests of the Arbs were religious in nature. It may be true that land, power and wealth were the primary aims but we can at least say without fear of contradiction that Islam was their inspiration and driving force and that Islam followed on the heels of military conquest and the promulgation of the faith was conducted with vigour everywhere the armies went.

But, in the early days, there was a problem. Mohammed was the only source for this new religion and he had not written down the revelations of God passed to him by the angel Gabriel. However, something had occurred which solved the problem. Over a period of time, many people approached Mohammed to ask what they should do in different circumstances and what God expected of them and Mohammed had answered them by reciting parts of what he had been told by Gabriel. These various people, we do not know how many, all wrote down the answers on whatever material they had to hand, stones, leaves etc. Some twenty years after Mohammed died, these scraps were collected together and collated into the Quran. It is accepted as true that Mohammed recalled every word of the Quran perfectly, that he recited it to his numerous followers perfectly, that they then wrote it perfectly, that every piece of scrap was kept for more than twenty years and every piece was found and the text was then re-written and compiled perfectly. This highly improbable story is seen as miraculous by Muslims and as one of the proofs that Islam is real.

Suggesting that a miracle, which itself cannot be proven, is proof that Islam is real is not seen as a problem by people who answer questions about the provenance of the Quran by referring to passages in the Quran which tell us that the book is true.

This collecting together of information from numerous sources is repeated later in the story of Islam and may be seen as a theme.

After the death of Mohammed, the followers of the Prophet and the new religion broke apart. Religious differences born from variations in the story of the Prophet and exacerbated by very human rivalries, caused internal strife and eventually a fracturing of Islam into two main sects, the Sunni and the much smaller Shia. These two later had many other offshoots but none of these problems are relevant to the main purpose here of examining the story itself.

The next element of the main story to concern us happened another 130 years after Mohammad died. The story goes that an oral history of the life of Muhammad had been maintained but not written down. This oral history was taught by a man named Ibn Ishaq and eventually committed to paper by a man called Al Bakka'i. Unfortunately, this incredibly important work was lost but an edited and redacted version had been written by a man called Ibn Hisham before he died in 833AD, two hundred years after the death of Mohammed and this document and later copies did survive. The Sira is considered to be vital to Muslims as all followers of Islam are expected to emulate the life of the Prophet. Again, the validity of the Sira is dependent upon the accuracy of the original oral history, the accuracy of the later written version and the accuracy of the second version as written by Ibn Hisham but these problems are not disputed by Muslims.

The story then moves forward another few years to a man named Al Bukhari. It seems that there were a great many stories going around which were purported to be authentic sayings of the Prophet and these sayings were believed, in varying degrees by Muslims. The problem was that many of them were contradictory or unbelievable. Al Bukhari took it upon himself to collect all of these sayings and wade through them to determine which were real and which were false. This done, he would collate them into a single book. But there was a problem. There were 600,000 of them.

By his death in 870AD, Al Bukhari had apparently read and assessed all 600,000. He discarded all but 7,000 as false and collected the correct ones into 9 volumes. (5,000 of the 7,000 he kept later turned out to be repeats) To demonstrate the Herculean nature of his task, the original 600,000 would have made 772 volumes. It may be observed that this story is, once again, questionable but, to Muslims, this very implausibility indicates that something miraculous must have happened.

Despite the sterling work done by Al Bukhari and his determination that only 7,000 of the 600,000 sayings of the Prophet were true, over the next 30 or 40 years a number of other men somehow came up with other sayings. These were all put together in what Muslims today call the Hadith. A hadith has two parts—the chain of narrators who have transmitted the report (the isnad), and the main text of the report (the matn). Individual hadith are classified by Muslim clerics and jurists into categories such as sahih (authentic), hasan (good) or da'if (weak). However, different groups and different scholars may classify a hadith differently. It must also be pointed out that some Muslims do not believe in the Hadith at all and state that only the Quran is important.

The above events are what mainstream Islam considers to be the most important and relevant. That they are hard to believe is, to Muslims, partly what makes them believable. All religions must, by their very nature, have an element of miracle and Islam is no different. It is not for me to pass judgement on whether these miracles, these deeply implausible events really took place but it must be admitted that seen without the filter of existing belief, they are hard to accept.

In summary;
Mohammed didn't write down what the angel had said.
He later used parts of what he had been told to answer questions from his followers.
Many of his followers, completely independently of each other and without any specific goal, wrote down his answers on stones and leaves.
These answers were all expertly heard and recorded and the versions that remain are perfect.
These answers on scraps were collected into the Quran years after Mohammed's death.
The life of Mohammed is to be the example for all Muslims for all time but it was only kept as an oral history.
When finally written down, 130 years after Mohammed's death, it was lost.
The edited and redacted copy completed around another 50 years later is, nonetheless, seen as authoritative.
600,000 sayings of the Prophet were circulated and, 250 years after Mohammed died, one man collected them all and decided which ones were real, on his own authority.
After this massive undertaking, more 'real' sayings were found by a number of other men.

Muslims would no doubt look at the above summary in horror and claim it misinterprets the truth or is made to portray events in a bad light but what I have done here is precisely what Muslims believe and Islam teaches. I have not invented anything, nor added undue stress to any event to make it seem more unlikely than the Islamic account. All I have done is related the bare facts, as taught.

These things seem reminiscent of the Christian's New Testament. They appear to be legends that have built up around a single figure who may or may not have existed. There are sceptics who claim that everything was invented in the medieval period, hundreds of years after the events described and that Mohammed never lived, just as some claim the same about Jesus but I think this is taking it too far.

It seems to me too incredible that everything is made up. Who would have done so and how would such an undertaking be possible? It must be remembered that at the time this invention supposedly took place, the Arab led Muslim war machine was already conquering as far afield as Spain and the borders of India. It cannot be denied that it was the fervent beliefs of these early Muslims that made them so resolved and so effective. I think it highly unlikely that such depth of feeling would exist surrounding a myth only recently invented. If we discount the Islamic tale itself, I think it more feasible that Mohammed was real, that he did claim a revelation and that from there a religion was built based on his teaching. I do, however, question the details of what it is claimed came next.

I am sorry if it offends, but the idea that hundreds of unconnected people wrote down perfectly what they were told by Mohammed, that these nuggets were later collected and that together they form the inerrant word of God is too much to accept. Likewise, the stories behind the biography and the sayings of the Prophet are equally impossible. These things simply could not have happened, as described, without miracle and without the direction of God and the existence of both is open to question.

The reason no Muslim has been able to convince me, in over 35 years of debating the point, is that without a belief in God, the miracles are impossible and so Islam is false. And it is only the belief in the miracles of Islam that makes the belief in God possible. It is circular reasoning. God exists because the Quran says so and the Quran is genuine because it is the word of God.

To end where I began, I cannot state with authority that what I have described above did not happen. I have no way to back that up. I merely state that it is deeply implausible, even impossible unless one already believes. To a Muslim, this is an indication that I have turned from God. Islam teaches that all men are born Muslim but many are unaware or turn away, which is why, when someone decides to become a Muslim, it is not called a conversion but a reversion.

Ultimately, with Islam as with every other religion, it is necessary to believe in the whole before you can believe in the details. I would suggest that if it were possible to raise children to the age of twenty-one with absolutely no knowledge of religion whatsoever and then present them with the basic, stripped-down facts claimed as truth by the various religions, the number of people who took up any particular faith would be small indeed.

WHAT IS THE BIBLE?

And is it true?

This article is not concerned with personal faith, nor does it explore the existence of God. By virtue of being a deeply personal feeling, it is impossible to disprove the faith of another. Similarly, there is no evidence that God exists nor, it must be said, does not exist. What follows is only about the Bible and the claims made for it.

The Bible, made up of the Old and New Testaments, is mainly seen as the holy book of Christianity. The Old Testament is a collection of smaller books which purport to tell the history of the world and of the Jewish people, from the creation of the earth by God, right up to 400 years before the arrival of Jesus of Nazareth. The New Testament is made up of four different versions of the life of Jesus, together with an account of the actions of his followers after his death and numerous letters between Paul, the first person to propose a new religion based around Jesus and early groups of believers in a number of cities in the classical world. It ends with a strange work of prophecy, the true meaning of which no-one had ever been able to agree.

There is much debate concerning the authorship and reliability of all of the books of the Bible. This problem is exacerbated by the fact that we do not possess any original versions of the books therein, only hand-written copies of other hand-written copies, which show many errors and deliberate changes. It should also be noted that the first full manuscripts we have of these books are dated from hundreds of years after the events they describe.

In the case of the New Testament, the four versions of the life of Jesus are known as the gospels, a word which itself has come to mean truth but which was originally derived from the Anglo-Saxon 'godspell', meaning good news or good telling. In fact, although Christians are expected to believe the gospels to be absolute truth, there is much reason to doubt. As mentioned, they vary greatly and we do not even know the true authors; the names they now bear did not appear on early manuscripts and were added later to make them appear as if written by Jesus' disciples and, presumably, to lend weight and authority.

The issue of whether the stories in the Bible are true or not is a fairly modern one, which would not have occurred to people at the time they were written. Today, we are familiar with history as an exacting, almost scientific discipline, which seeks out and recounts a series of facts about a life, an event or a period of time, but this was not always so. Ancient historians saw their task very differently. To them the purpose of their work was the overall message not the reliability of every detail. Thus, the Greek historian Herodotus has been called both the Father of History and the Father of Lies. When we read ancient tales of gods and men, of wonderous achievements and of events which gave meaning to something which happened many years later, we are not reading a series of real occurrences but a story, designed to provide an overall theme. The word 'history' evolved from a Greek verb meaning to seek knowledge but to the Greeks of the classical era, knowledge meant more than simple facts and in Latin, 'historia' means both history and story.

What Christians call the Old Testament is in fact the Tanakh of the Jewish religion but with the order of the books altered. In the original form, the first five books, the Torah, traditionally called the books of Moses, are in the same order but the rest are grouped together as Nevi'im (Prophets) and Ketuvim (Writings). As a whole, the Tanakh is taken to be a history of the Jewish people. It begins with God's creation of the world and some tales of early humans and then tells a large number of stories with a common theme; when the people honour God, they prosper and when they turn away from God, they are punished. There are prophets who repeatedly accuse the people of their transgressions and who predict disaster, which then happens, usually through invasion by a larger nation. The invaders are sent by God, even if they don't realise it themselves and actually worship a completely different set of gods. The books of the Tanakh were collated and edited during the most significant of these disasters, when the Jews were conquered by the Babylonians and the people, or at least the upper sections of society, were taken into captivity in Babylon. The whole Tanakh may therefore be seen as an effort to preserve tradition and to give the people hope.

The New Testament is purely a Christian work. Jewish and Islamic traditions acknowledge Jesus as a major prophet but absolutely deny his divinity. The concept of a messiah was first a Jewish one. The word simply means 'anointed one' and all the kings and religious leaders of the Jews were anointed with oil. The Christians adopted the term and gave it to Jesus, re-defined to mean a divine figure who has come and will return to usher in the Kingdom of God. The Jewish messiah, in contrast, was initially seen as an earthly and secular figure who will eventually save the Jewish people from their oppressors, although around the time of Jesus there were messianic Jews who had developed the divine messiah idea. When Cyrus the Great of Persia defeated the Babylonians and allowed the Jews to return to their homeland, he was referred to as the messiah in the Bible. After that the idea changed somewhat to mean a new messiah, still a man, who will rebuild the temple in Jerusalem and rescue the Jews. The Jewish messiah is yet to come. It cannot be Jesus because he did not do what the messiah is expected to do.

The New Testament tells the story of Jesus and a little of what followed his death. The gospels were written between 20 and 100 years after the death of Jesus and whilst taken to be literal truth by some Christians, they may be more accurately be seen as works of faith, not history. Jesus apparently promised that he would return to bring the kingdom of God before any of his followers died but this didn't happen. It seems likely that the gospels represent the various oral traditions that had built up about Jesus and that they were written down to preserve them and to aid in spreading the faith. Something that the early followers of Jesus, all Jews, would not have needed because they were waiting for his expected and imminent return. This idea, of works of faith, is supported by the strange and marked differences in the gospels. If they are all accurate and truly tell of some of the most significant events in human history, there shouldn't be any discrepancies at all but, in reality, we see a great many. Even though it may be demonstrated that the gospels of Matthew and Luke are word for word copies of 90% of the gospel of Mark, where they do depart from their source material, they offer very different accounts. The gospel of John is even more distinct. Clearly written much later and in a very different style, it paints a totally different picture of Jesus. No longer a man with a divine mission, he is now not only godlike, he is at once God's son and a part of God. He is strong, unwavering and full of his purpose.

The vast majority of religious believers around the world see the Bible as inspired by God. Written by unknown men but men carrying a burden placed on them by God to tell his story. In addition, there exist a far smaller number of people who believe the Bible to be literally the word of God and that its authors were merely God's instruments in setting down a completely accurate and inerrant account of the events and people therein. Whichever camp an individual chooses for themselves, or are born and inculcated into, they face a number of problems when trying to defend their position and to convince others.

Firstly, there is no external evidence to support any of the events in the old or new testaments. We know of some towns and cities and a very small number of people, from extrabiblical sources but nothing else and absolutely nothing to support any Bible story. There is a stone stele which refers to King David but it tells us only that he lived, not what he did. The same is true of some of the kings at the very end or most recent parts of the story. In fact, archaeologists have found much that casts doubt, such as evidence of a continual Canaanite culture in the 'promised land' with nothing to show an invasion by conquering Israelites. There have been many Canaanite temples unearthed but not one for a people with a single God.

With modern science and a level of knowledge of the world and the universe which was unavailable to the authors, we now know and can prove, that the creation story in the Bible is not only wrong, it is impossible. The same is true of Noah's ark, the tower of Babel and the exodus. These impossibilities are irrelevant if the Bible is a mythologised history of a people but they are a profound problem if we are to believe the Bible is true.

The New Testament, despite being set in a more recent time, suffers from the same problems. It tells us that when Jesus was born, King Herod ruled the land, as a client king of the Romans and Quirinius was the Roman Governor of Syria. Unfortunately, whilst both of these figures were real people, we have contemporary records which show they were not in place at the same time but were separated by 9 years. Similarly, the Bible portrays Governor Pontius Pilate as a reasonable man who is unwilling to condemn Jesus but again contemporary Roman records show that he was a deeply unpleasant character who liked to abuse his power and was actually rebuked by Rome for being too cruel and unjust to the Jews, thereby causing civil unrest.

As previously mentioned, the gospels contain many discrepancies, far too many to list here. They range from who carried the cross, to Jesus' last words, what happened as Jesus died and even who found Jesus' empty tomb, what they saw there and what they did next. One particularly puzzling event is recounted in Matthew. It tells us that when Jesus died, there was an earthquake and the dead rose from their graves and walked the streets of Jerusalem, being seen by many. And yet not only was this incredible thing, this horrifying spectacle of a zombie apocalypse, not recorded by the Romans, even the other gospels fail to mention something so utterly amazing.

So, why are Christians in particular so adamant that the Bible is true, either literally or at least in overall reliability?

The problem arose when Christianity changed the nature of the Old Testament. What was a mythical or semi-mythical story of a people, designed to provide hope in captivity and to demonstrate a pattern of what happened when they turned away from God, became simply a precursor to the arrival and purpose of Jesus. Christians at the time of writing the gospels and ever since, have referred back to passages in the Old Testament, some obscure, some clearly meant to be prophecy of something and they have claimed them as prophecies of Jesus Christ. Unfortunately, in every single instance, the claims lack merit. Either the passage is too vague to be considered prophecy at all or it may be shown to relate to something closer to its own time and far more relevant and convincing than a link to Jesus.

The gospels actually say that things happened so that prophecy might be fulfilled. Christians take this to mean circumstances were arranged, by God, in order to meet the prophecy but it is far more likely that Jesus and his followers deliberately manipulated events to match their existing knowledge of the old scriptures.

In the final analysis, the biggest problem of the Bible rests not with the authors intentions but in the way later Christians employed it. Instead of emphasizing a tradition of Jesus' teachings and linking them to personal faith, which cannot be argued against, they placed so much emphasis on its accuracy that, for Christianity itself to be considered viable, the Bible *must* be true. In its original form, the overall message is not harmed by challenging individual facts but in Christianity's version, the whole must be true or Jesus is not true. As we have often seen, the Bible cannot support such a burden.

THE DEFINITION OF ARROGANCE

Why the fine-tune argument is nonsense.

Until the Enlightenment began in the mid seventeen hundreds, the only generally accepted version of how life, the universe and everything came to be, was that put forward by religion. Of course, the details of that argument were dependant entirely on which god one believed in but for our purpose I will stick to the monotheistic god; the God at the centre of the three Abrahamic faiths, Judaism, Christianity and Islam.

The primary source material for these religions is the Bible or, more specifically, the collection of books known to Christians as The Old Testament. In it, the first book, Genesis, provides an account of how everything was created by God in six days (In fact there are two versions pushed together, with different and conflicting orders of events).

For centuries, without science to provide an alternative viewpoint and without the means to see beyond the sky, there was little reason to doubt the assertion, God did it. Indeed, early astronomers like Copernicus and Galileo were put on trial and punished by the church for daring to propose that the earth was not the very centre of the universe around which the sun and everything else revolved.

Back when the Christian church ruled a dark age and medieval Europe with an iron hand and the threat of divine retribution, human progress in science and technology was discouraged, because everything mankind needed to know was in the Bible; the literal word of God. Any thinking which did not conform was both heretical and pointless, because Jesus had promised to return to usher in The Kingdom of God. We cannot know how much our advancement as a species may have been retarded by such oppression and we must thank the scholars of Islam for preserving the thoughts of the Greek and Roman philosophers and for, at least in part, continuing their work.

Today, we can see further and think more clearly and religion has lost its stranglehold on our minds. But what do religious apologists do to defend the crumbling foundations of their belief system, when science provides a vast array of knowledge about the universe and ourselves? New, more sophisticated arguments must be found to counter this tidal wave of information and knowledge, lest the old ways be swept away.

Keep in mind that for those whom God is very real and the core of their world view and their whole lives, simply abandoning their faith is close to impossible. It is certainly not something on which they are prepared to keep an open mind. How could they? Instead, preachers and apologists look at all of this new information and they try to find answers for it. They misrepresent science to their flock, lie about the nature of truth and fact and try to prove the existence of God. Something that has never before been required.

There are a great many supposed 'proofs'. Sadly, for these people of faith, every single one of them has been refuted many times. And yet they persist. The internet carries so many sites dedicated to showing that science is wrong and religion is right. The intensity of them varies between those that believe the Bible to be, quite literally, the inerrant word of God, accurate and true in every detail, to those who take the Bible only as inspiration but still believe in God the creator.

The more science expands our understanding of the universe, the more elaborate and detailed are the counter arguments. One such is the idea is that the universe is fine-tuned to favour life, specifically human life and that, if a handful of scientific principals were even slightly adjusted, life would be impossible. This notion is actually a development from an earlier and equally well-used proposition, that of intelligent design.

The argument has been put forward in many ways but one of the most famous is that of the English clergyman William Paley. In 1802, he wrote that if he found a watch on the ground it would be reasonable to presume that it had been made by a watchmaker. It would be far too complex to be a natural phenomenon. So it is with everything we see around us. Therefore, the universe and everything in it must have been designed, by God.

Over time, many holes have been found in this argument. For example, even if we accept the basic principle, why must the designer be Abraham's God? Why not Odin or Brahman, Zeus or Baal? The most fundamental challenge to Paley's idea, however, developed later. Whilst it may have been a struggle to defend the watchmaker analogy in 1802, it is impossible today, simply because we know so much more about how things actually work. In other words, we now live in a universe of watches. We actually possess evidence of how complexity may arise from simplicity.

The watchmaker argument began to fade but was given a fresh lease of life when science began to uncover a number of physical laws, or constants, which seem to dictate how the universe operates. Things like gravity, the speed of light and entropy; the rate at which organisation or cosmos, devolves into chaos. It was determined by scientists, that if any of these constants were changed by even a small degree, the universe would be a very different place and life, as we understand it, would be impossible. In fact, scientists now understand that the formation of galaxies, stars and planets would be impossible. Religious apologists jumped on this news with undisguised glee. It was now clear, they claimed, that God really did create the universe, because if he had not made it in precisely the way he did, we would not be here to discover his truth.

At this point, many apologists fold their arms, sit back and smile smugly. Job done. But is it?

Firstly, the idea that a complex and seemingly fragile set of laws must have been intelligently designed does not hold true. It rests upon a different and even older assertion by the religious lobby; the cosmological argument, often referred to as the

Kalam argument, named after an Islamic scholarly document. It goes as follows:

Whatever begins to exist must have a cause.

The universe exists.

The universe must have had a beginning.

Therefore, the universe had a cause, which must lie outside of itself.

That cause is God.

Unfortunately for the argument, it is, again, full of holes. The first, is the premise that the universe had a beginning and is not itself infinite and eternal. Another is that God must be the cause. But the biggest flaw is that it is tripped-up by its own logic. It stops with God but if we follow the logic through, we must state that God must have had a beginning and therefore a cause and we must ask, who created God? From there we are trapped in an infinite regression. The argument rests upon clear logical steps that seem irrefutable but, once it reaches God, it demands that its own clear logic is abandoned. This is simply a convenience prompted by intellectual dishonesty.

To return to the fine-tuned argument. If there is one attribute that scientists have, which distinguishes them from religious apologists, it is a willingness to be proven wrong. Whilst religions require adherence to dogma and speak in certainties, scientists fully accept that science is a process and one in which we learn more as time passes and new discoveries often change what we thought we knew. Right now, scientists think that the laws of physics, as they are known colloquially, are fixed across the universe, but that may change. It will most assuredly change in the details. There is a hypothesis that our own universe might incorporate regions with different characteristics. Another, that there was not a single Big Bang but many, all creating universes with differing criteria. And yet another, where our universe eventually ends in a quantum energy field and that a fluctuation in this field will give rise to the next Big Bang, and so on infinitum.. It follows then, that to assert that these laws prove a designer is, at the very least, premature. But even if we accept that the physical constants we have observed are fixed and fine-tuned, it does not automatically require a tuner.

We have used the Hubble telescope to see farther and farther into the universe and further back in time. Because light travels at a fixed speed in a vacuum, once we know how far away a distant star is, we also know how long it has taken the light from it to reach us. E.g. light from our sun takes 8 minutes to reach earth. If aliens stole our sun, we would not know about it for 8 minutes (I'm ignoring gravity for the sake of brevity). In this way, the deeper we look into the universe, the further back in time we go. We are presently able to determine what happened just after the perceived formation of the universe; often known as The Big Bang. Because time itself is a function of the universe, it is impossible to go any further back. We cannot therefore know exactly how the universe came to be.

The term Big Bang was first coined as mockery and it is true to say that we do not know if such a thing actually happened. Because we cannot see all the way back to the supposed beginning of our universe, it may be that we have it wrong and the beginning was more like a fresh start for an older universe, possibly in an unending chain or as part of a multitude of other universes.

Religious people are no longer able to claim, as was previously the case, that God lives in a Heaven just beyond the sky, as the Bible tells us but they still assert that God created everything. Some claim it happened as the Bible says, others that God used the laws of physics. But there are other explanations, just as plausible.

Perhaps the universe is eternal, without need of a creator; locked in a continual cycle, with new universes possibly having the same laws, possibly different.

Or perhaps there are an infinite number of universes, a

multiverse, where every possible combination of laws exists and only in a tiny number is there any life.

Or perhaps life is the ultimate expression of a vast computer programme called the universe, designed by aliens so large that we exist as the smallest possible form of life.

Or perhaps we all exist in The Matrix.

The point is that every one of these ideas is equally as likely as any other and that they all, including the God hypothesis, possess the same level of proof. None.

But, for me, there is a larger problem with the idea that the universe was created by God with us in mind. The staggering arrogance of it.

Keep in mind that the earliest source material we have for a belief in the God of Abraham, is the Bible. And the Bible gives a very clear explanation as to how and why the universe was created by God. He did it in 6 days. He created the heavens and the earth. He made light and separated night from day. Only after doing that, did he create the sun and the moon (Ricky Gervais joked about how clever God was because he created the Earth, *in the dark!*"). He created a dome to separate the waters above from the waters beneath and he called the dome the sky. The Bible describes the 'firmament' as a solid thing, polished to shine and possessing windows to let in the water above as rain. He gathered the water together and dry land appeared. God made lights to mark day and night and he made the stars and he set them in the dome. He then went on to make life in various forms but we can leave it there. The point is made. The sun, the moon and the stars were placed in the dome of the sky and everything else was done expressly in order to lead up to the ultimate creation, us.

I want to provide a few facts and figures at this point. They will not be boring. They may just blow your mind.

You know the universe is big, but it is way bigger than you think.

It's bigger than human minds can grasp.

The sun is 864,000 miles (1,392,000 km) in diameter, which makes it 109 times wider than Earth.
If the sun were the size of a pea, the earth would not be visible to the naked eye. The orbit of Neptune would still be 3.5 miles away from the pea.
At the same scale, the nearest star, Proxima Centauri would be 125 miles (202 km) away from the pea.
Betelgeuse, the size of a car compared to our pea-like sun, would be approximately 30 thousand miles away.

But, as mind boggling as these distances are, they don't even hint at the size of the universe.

The Large Magellanic Cloud is one of the galaxies closest to our own and actually seems to be in orbit around the Milky Way. It is approx. 200,000 light years away. That is to say the light from it, which travels at well over 670 million miles per hour, takes 200,000 years to reach us.

The farthest galaxy we have found, so far, is 13.2 billion light years away. That means we are seeing that galaxy not as it is but as it was, billions of years ago.

In the mid-nineties, the Hubble telescope photographed a particularly dark area of space, about the size of a pea held at arm's length. In that 'deep field image' they found something incredible. Thousands of distant galaxies. Extrapolating from that count, it has been estimated that there are around 200 billion galaxies in the known universe, each one holding millions of individual stars.
70% of stars studied so far have planets in orbit and, strictly as an average, there is a planet for every star.

Because of the distances involved, we truly have no idea what the universe actually looks like today. We are seeing our *nearest* neighbouring galaxy as it was two hundred thousand years ago.

We have no idea how big the universe really is. We can estimate the size of the visible universe (not actually visible to us but technically possible to see with better equipment) but it may stretch much much further.

As an interesting aside; our sun is so small and dim and insignificant, compared to other stars out there, that its light would not be visible from more than 100 light years away.

Let's return to our own solar system and consider colonising other worlds. It has been suggested that the moons of Jupiter might be a possibility but there is a problem. Because of the different speeds of the orbits of Earth and Jupiter, the distance between them varies from 365 million miles to 601 million miles. If we travel too slow, we might miss our aim, too fast we would be unable to stop. At a safe velocity it would currently take us 6 years to get there. And that's our own neighbourhood. After we eventually colonise other planets in our own solar system, in terms of interstellar travel, we haven't even left the house.
Unless we develop faster than light travel, or borrow it from aliens, there is no easy way to visit other planets and no possible way to visit other solar systems. Faster than light travel is impossible, as far as we know right now.

I told you it was big.

Another fact is that, with the exception of hydrogen, every atom of every element on earth, including those that make up all humans, came from the immense explosions of dying stars. These heavy elements, as scientists call them, are not found anywhere else in the universe. This means that for us to exist at all, at least one star had to be born from a collection of interstellar gas, explode into life, burn for millions of years, turning hydrogen into helium, only to die in a catastrophic explosion. It would have had to be one of the bigger stars, our own is nowhere near large enough. This catastrophic death was necessary in order to create heavier elements and expel them into the universe to be later coalesced by gravity into our sun and its children.

All of the above facts have been discovered and proven to be accurate with thorough and repeated testing by hundreds of individuals over many decades. And yet religious people still believe, or are expected to believe, that God created the universe, *for us*, as described in the Bible.

Even if we presume the Bible to be merely a human interpretation of cosmic events and that God really is the creator, although in a very different way, it begs a question. Why would an omniscient, omnipotent god come up with something so vast, so wasteful and so deadly to all life, simply to make us? Something more local and more simple must have been a better option.

The truth is that the existence of God cannot be proven, nor disproven. It is impossible to provide any meaningful evidence for something which may or may not exist outside our universe and is also undetectable to our senses. God's existence must be taken on faith and faith is, by definition, belief without evidence. For this reason alone, all attempts to prove God are futile. Attempts to do so by using science are a waste of time.

The fine-tuned universe argument fails in its details as mentioned above, but it fails mainly because its assumptions are solipsistic and supremely arrogant. To imagine that the vast and complex universe exists and has existed for billions of years, simply in order that our sun might begin to burn, our earth might be formed, life might spring forth, humans might find themselves at the top of the food chain, with the brain power and time to think about such problems and that the creator of all of this did it so that he could have a personal relationship with a small section of one particular species, is simply laughable.

And when, in the fullness of time, an asteroid large enough to wipe out all life on earth is discovered heading towards us, or our sun goes nova, are we to simply accept it as God's will? Do we try to find a solution or do we kneel and pray for salvation?

GOD IS GOOD

Let me set out my stall early. Whilst I usually choose not to define myself with a negative, I am an atheist. More than that, I am an anti-theist. Not only do I not believe in any form of deity, if the God of Abraham did exist, whether he wanted to be called God, Yahweh or Allah, I don't think we would get along.

I have read his instructions and his expectations in the holy books and I have witnessed what he has done and encouraged or allowed his followers to do to one another over the centuries and he just doesn't seem like my kind of person. But maybe I'm just too sensitive to things like genocide, the ritual mutilation of children's genitals and a death sentence for anyone who is rude to their parents, wears the wrong clothes, ploughs a field in the wrong way or wants to jump-ship and worship him with new friends. Of which more later.

There. I have been honest about my affiliation. I hope you will read on.

All of the above issues I have with God could be attributed to mistranslation or a corruption of the message by humans. Something I have heard often from apologists. Except, if God does exist, why would he allow such mistakes to occur and why would he allow millions of deaths and terrible persecution over thousands of years, based on those errors? I know a great many religious believers place faith above logic but these questions seem to be pretty basic objections. The only answers to these questions that I have encountered are, *"God works in mysterious ways"* or *"It is not given to us to know the mind of God"* and the old favourite, *"God gave us free will"*. None of which are really answers, only ways of dodging the issue.

One of the things that I find difficult to comprehend is the hypocrisy of the monotheistic faiths. Jews, Muslims and Christians all acknowledge that there is one God and that they all worship the same one. They all proclaim that God is all-knowing, all-seeing, all-powerful etc. God is the creator of the universe but still takes a daily interest in the lives of every human being and damnation waits for those who break the rules. And yet they insist upon hating, persecuting and killing each other in the name of that same God. God commands them to love each other but also, apparently, expects them to kill for the cause. And they just don't see the dichotomy. God also allows, or even instructs, people to worship him in very different ways, even though this is guaranteed to cause conflict. Is he a sadist or does he just have a twisted sense of humour?

Muslims answer this question by pointing out that Jews and Christians were given a chance but they went astray and so God sent the angel Gabriel to Mohammed to dictate the truth, the real way he wants us to behave. The problem with this view is that there is no evidence to show that the behaviour of Jews changed drastically over the centuries or that the Christians began well and went wrong. But, perhaps more importantly, why did God wait for centuries whilst the Jews were getting it wrong before sending Jesus to be sacrificed to him and then why did he wait another 600 years to step in again and try to put things right and why do it in such a way as to cause centuries of bloodshed?

It may be said that all this is caused by human error but we keep returning to the same question; why would God allow it? He is God after all, surely he could allow us free will and still educate us in how best to use it? Or at least be clear about what he wants.

At this point I have to say that my comments are not a criticism of any one religion. In these troubled times it is easy for Christians and Jews to claim that they are peaceful but Islam is not the religion of peace it is purported to be. I'm afraid that this is either ignorance or wilful blindness to the truth. Those Jews and Christians that feel themselves morally superior to Muslims either know nothing of their own history, or they think that being separated by a few years from atrocities committed in the name of God is a good enough excuse. Islam has many millions of followers who abhor violence and live honest, peaceful lives, as does Judaism and Christianity but it must be said that these people, from all three faiths, are able to do so only by cherry picking the parts of their holy books they wish to follow. Moderates accuse fundamentalists of misusing the holy texts and fundamentalists accuse the moderates of the same, but the truth is that both are guilty of ignoring the parts they don't agree with.

Jesus of Nazareth said that he came not to change the old law, but to fulfil it. Before Saul of Tarsus had his conversion on the road to Damascus, changed his name and began preaching to gentiles, Jesus and his family and friends were proclaiming his word only to Jews. At one point, Jesus refused to help a non-Jew and used the analogy of not giving your child's food to a dog. This vile notion seems to pass Christians by, as did Jesus' referring to those who would not follow him as dogs and pigs and his admonition to hate your family and to abandon them to follow him. Even while Paul was writing to early Christians in other cities, Jew and gentile, the original followers of Jesus were true to his message, that he had come to bring the Jews back to God. Logically therefore, Christians are bound by the incredible and often horrific laws of behaviour in the Old Testament and, like the Jews, are equal inheritors of the genocide and other appalling crimes committed by God and by Joshua and others under God's specific instruction.

By his own words, Jesus came to fulfil the old laws and God decreed that the sins of the father shall be passed on to his children and his children's children. So, are not the Christians also bound by the old laws? Should they not bear equal responsibility to excuse the abhorrent crimes in the Old Testament?
Incidentally, can you think of any human law that punishes children and grandchildren for the crimes of the forebears? What a vile, morally bankrupt idea.

Jesus told his listeners to give no thought for tomorrow but just follow him; to hate and leave their parents and do what he instructed. He also stated that he was here not to bring peace but a sword. And, just in case some were tempted not to obey his words to the letter, Christian followers of the God of love invented the concept of everlasting damnation. Before Jesus, you could be enslaved, raped, beaten and killed if God so wished it, but at least death was an end of suffering. The followers of Jesus decided that you could burn for eternity for your sins. Even new-born babies that had not been baptised were destined for the fires. Has there ever been a more unpleasant doctrine?

I am, of course, being ridiculous. Christians do not obey all these awful instructions and examples in the Bible, any more than do the Jews. The very idea is laughable. But why not?

All religious people cherry pick. That is a simple truth. If we begin with the premise that the Bible and the Quran are the word of God, put into men's minds so that they may spread the message, we must accept that not one single person has ever followed those words religiously, if you will pardon the rather obvious pun. All the holy books of the Abrahamic faiths are so filled with internal inconsistencies and contradictions, it is simply impossible that they *could* be followed to the letter.

Some people choose the violent parts of their holy books to support their actions and justify mind-numbing barbarity, for causes that are usually more to do with politics and greed than actual faith. Thankfully, many more choose to ignore those violent instructions and other unpleasant parts of the books, in order to live in the modern world. Clearly the latter are easier to understand and live with, but both are guilty of making choices of which their God clearly would not approve and, presumably, did not intend.

Here I would cite the Westboro Baptist church in the USA. Members of this congregation, whilst being nominally Christian, are so outside of what most people consider Christian behavior that they campaign with placards and shouted slogans which are deeply offensive to many. They meet the coffins of fallen soldiers with cries of "baby killer" and "happy your son is dead", they claim that all gay people will burn in hell and they state that the whole world has fallen for Satan's lies and only they are the true Christians. One placard reads, "You will eat your babies", which sounds vile, but is actually a quote from the Bible, with only a small change (Leviticus 26:29 *And ye shall eat the flesh of your sons, and the flesh of your daughters shall ye eat*"). As disgusting as most people find their actions, who is to say they are not right? They take their instruction and their quotes directly from the Bible, so who can say, with certainty, that they are not doing God's will and it is all other Christians who have it wrong? After all, in the Bible, God committed genocide and, in other instances, killed many thousands, as well instructing others to do the same, so the actions of the Westboro Baptists are not far from the examples offered by God.

But what if we don't believe that these books are without error? What if we choose to believe that the holy books are merely written by men *inspired* by a belief in God? This sounds a better option, as it allows for honest mistakes in understanding, recitation and translation, but this too is problematic.

If the books are open to human fallibility, where precisely are the errors? Which bits *do* we follow to the letter? Which *do* we take as merely metaphor? How do we interpret those parts that are unclear? Which do we ignore? And, more importantly, who is qualified to make such decisions and with what authority?

The Christian Bible, incorporating the old and the new testaments, is presented to us today as a single book, or more accurately, two books linked together. But those two books, seemingly homogenous, have been edited and altered, numerous times, by groups of men who decided which texts should be included and which left out. Their decisions have had a profound effect on the way Christians and Jews understand their own history and faith, but by what authority did they make their choice? Is the will of God to be decided by committee?

We may feel that it is for the conscience of every man to decide for himself whether his personal values and morals allow him to obey certain instructions and ignore others. But if this is so, it allows for as many versions of a religion as there are people on earth. In this scenario there is no single truth, therefore the whole concept is worthless. We are left merely with billions of versions of personal faith.

Or we may feel that a hierarchy is required to guide the faithful. A church which can teach certain doctrines and keep people on the straight and narrow. But who chooses these leaders? Are they merely picked at random and educated in orthodoxy to give them authority, or are they first chosen by God and given the internal urge to join? If they are simply better educated versions of you and me, how can we trust that their understanding is correct? If they, or their sponsors, claim them to be chosen by God, how do we know that is the truth? The fact is, we don't know. We are simply expected to believe and to obey.

The election of a new Pope in the Vatican is a case in point. All the Cardinals gather together and they vote. They repeat the vote as many times as necessary until a clear winner is found, presumably with much discussion and persuasion along the way. But once the new Pope has been elected, Catholics are supposed to believe that he is chosen by God and is now empowered to speak in God's name.

However strong our personal faith, how can we know the hierarchy and rules of our religion are not just a trick, to maintain the power of a minority over the majority?

Islam does not have a hierarchy as such. Instead, it has scholars. Men who have spent their lives learning and studying the Quran, the Hadiths and the Sira; the commentary and explanations of the Quran, the sayings of Mohammed and the life of the Prophet. Whilst there are many of these men and they do not all agree, the same criticism can be levelled as that made above. How do we know their word may be trusted? They may or may not be honest, but they may also be honestly mistaken. This question becomes increasingly relevant when scholars differ widely in their interpretations and rulings and even attack one another's words. And more so when a scholar announces some crazy new ruling that the whole world can see is nonsense. Has such a man lost his authority to speak in God's name or did he never have it?

Leaving established religion to one side for a moment and despite my own atheism, I maintain that personal faith is not necessarily a bad thing. Deciding that your values are more important than surrendering to every temptation, may make you unpopular with your less committed neighbours but if it makes you love and honour people and the world in general there can be little harm. Of course, if your values tell you to hurt people or that others simply do not matter, that is completely different. You may be a psychopath or a sociopath and you clearly need help.

But, leaving aside mental illness and staying with a dedication to excellent personal values, the fact remains that, however good your intentions, the moment your values tell you that you have the right, or the duty, to convince others to follow you, things change.

If you believe a light bulb is channelling the spirit of Napoleon to tell you to give up meat, wash eight times a day and pray standing on your head, it is none of my business. If the light bulb is whispering '*kill them, kill them all*' we have a problem.

But what if your light bulb is giving you only good thoughts but backed up with an instruction to convince others to follow you and that you have the authority to tell others how to live? The moment you step outside and begin speaking, you are starting a religion and ultimately, no matter how sincere individuals may be, religion is more about control and power than it is about faith.

A story tells us that long ago a man called Abram was born in Ur of the Chaldees, in modern day Iraq, not that far from Basra. God told him to move to Canaan, change his name to Abraham and that, despite his advancing years, he would become the father of a great nation. Now, if we accept the story at all, we have no reason to doubt that Abraham truly believed he was speaking with a god; there being no dispute at the time that there were other gods around.

So far so good. But later on, Abraham's god told him to take his son out into the hills and sacrifice him. The old man so believed in his god that he was prepared to do it. At the last moment his god stopped him. It was all a test of faith and Abraham had passed. Followers of Abraham's god have accepted this ever since and some even praise God for sending the new instruction in the nick of time. Some of them may have questioned just how cruel and unnecessary this awful trick really was, but as a group they accept that God always knows best.

Those of us who do not believe, cannot understand why any all-knowing deity would need to impose such a test. If he was truly omniscient, he surely knew the heart of Abraham already? If he needed to test Abraham, is he really God? Believers will say that we cannot understand the ways of God. We could leave it there but then we see, in a book either written by God or at least on his behalf and inspired by him, that he is capable of far more horror than a tasteless practical joke.

The point I am labouring here is that, whilst a well-meaning personal faith is no bad thing, religion most assuredly is. Religious dogma doesn't need to be logical and it doesn't need to make sense. It has the authority granted it by your belief. Belief not only in your particular god, but in the ability and the right of the church, or a book or a scholar, to speak in God's name.

That authority and the blind obedience it demands, gives certain individuals immense power.

In medieval times the Catholic church could crown and dethrone kings. Today, in the USA, a country founded on religious freedom and the separation of church and state, we see hard-right Christians exerting increasing influence on government and cynical politicians appealing to the Christians in order to bolster their position. Evolution is being taught as merely an opinion and creationism is taught as science. Millions of children have their genitals mutilated; we balk at how it is done to girls but blithely accept the practice on boys. We have compulsory prayer in schools and churches being given the legal right to employ their own police. In the UK, Muslims have been allowed to exercise their own Sharia, a legal system based on man's interpretation of God's will, rather than any sense of justice, equality or human rights. As I write this, the laws of the land supersede religious laws but for how much longer? In many parts of the world, we see blasphemy laws upheld and promoted by the United Nations, at the insistence of Pakistan and other Muslim countries which take a more fundamentalist approach to Islam but with the support of the Vatican and American Christians. In real terms that is a 'would be' world government telling nation states to legislate against free speech and to punish those who speak out against religion. We should all be profoundly worried by these trends.

Christianity is almost 2000 years old, Islam around 600 years more recent. Despite the blinkers often worn by Christian critics of Muslims today, their own religion was once red with blood up to its elbows. And yet, with certain minor exceptions, Christianity has moved on, evolved, if you will allow the term. Islam too has changed. Sadly and worryingly, it has abandoned its golden age, when the Islamic world represented mankind's best in terms of science and philosophy and it now seems to yearn for a return to the desert of fourteen hundred years ago.

So, we see that religion, whilst still centred on the exercise of control and power, can change. It can become more gentle, more humanistic and less about killing your neighbour because he worships the same god in a different way. But it is also capable of going the other way. What is troubling is a resurgence of radicalism and fundamentalism; beginning with Islam but being matched, in spirit if not yet in action, by Christians.

In both religions there is a belief in millenarianism; a conviction that society is soon to change and that a new order will rise. The end of days. The apocalypse. Again, we return to cherry picking. Of course, most people don't think about such things, even if they vaguely acknowledge that their religion accepts it. The fundamentalists don't just think about it, they embrace it eagerly.

Even as some Muslims truly believe that they will be rewarded in heaven for killing non-believers, there are Christians who see a catastrophic, perhaps nuclear, war in the middle east as the necessary precursor to the return of Jesus Christ and the coming of God's kingdom and they collect money to support Israeli expansion into Palestinian lands in the hope that this might bring about Armageddon. If this seems extreme, keep in mind that the whole premise of Christianity, seen in the Sermon On The Mount, is that this world doesn't matter because a better one is coming. To these people, the violent end of everything we hold dear is the ultimate victory and such a conflict is to be welcomed and encouraged. We must be aware of such people and we should be afraid and on our guard.

Religious conflict will never, can never, be settled by religious people. They believe too hard. Take Islamic Jihadists as an example. To us they may seem insane, but they are the most deeply committed of their co-religionists. They are honestly prepared to give their lives and even the lives of their children to further what they truly know in their hearts to be God's cause.

Facing them we have Christians who believe, just as deeply, in their own truth, even if their holy book does not advocate martyrdom. They know, without any allowance of doubt, that everyone who does not follow their narrow interpretation of the Bible and the teachings of their elders, is a sinner against God and will be consigned to eternal flame. Some of them freely admit that they are only a hair's breadth away from making it happen themselves; taking direct action to bring on Armageddon. Understand that these people do not fear death, or the end of the world. They welcome it. Indeed, they are eagerly looking forward to it. Are we suitably afraid of these people?

The vast majority of Muslims, Jews and Christians, of course, do not think in this way and are appalled by the very idea. And yet they pray to the same God, read the same holy books and listen to the same teachings. Whilst they may not choose to be associated with the radicals, they are part of a contiguous community. The nutters, as we might call them, could not exist without the very same religions that the moderates follow.

Religion has always caused and will always cause conflict. Where we once killed in the name of our gods with clubs and swords, bows and arrows, we now use guided missiles, tanks and machine guns. It is only a matter of time before we see the use of chemical, biological and nuclear weapons in religious conflict.

In 1995 a group called Aum Shinrikyo used Sarin nerve gas on innocent people in the Tokyo underground. They were a religious group with a belief system based on Buddhism, one of the most peaceful philosophies ever devised but this group incorporated elements of Shivan Hindusim and, crucially, Christian millenarianism. Their leader actually called himself Christ and The Lamb of God. They killed 12 people, severely injured 50 more and caused partial blindness in nearly 5,000 others. All in the name of religion. They were trying to replace the Emperor of Japan with their leader, as this would allow him to bring on Armageddon.

Were they insane? Not in any medically accepted sense. They simply believed.

In conclusion, I would suggest that any of the established religions is as good, or as bad, as any other as the right way to follow God. However, the god they follow is clearly not good and following him, in any way, is a mistake. If this sounds shocking or harsh, allow me to clarify.

In the Old Testament, God specifically orders killing, incest, genital mutilation, genocide, slavery and sacrifice. He created humans with the capacity for sin, gave them free will and then punished them for being true to the nature he gave them. In what can only be termed a temper tantrum, he wiped out almost all life on earth, because he was angry with one species. We are expected to believe that 900 year old Noah and his kin were the only decent people in the whole world and we really shouldn't care about the billions of people, secretive squirrels, playful cats, loyal dogs, weird kangaroos and comical penguins that drowned. God then miraculously allowed for Noah's sons to repopulate the planet in an incredibly short period of time, giving rise to Kalahari bushmen, Chinese, Eskimos and Europeans and people who spoke hundreds of different languages. He ordered Abraham to sacrifice his son and allowed the torture of poor old Job, just to check the depth of his faith. All this from a being who is not only the creator of all things, but who already knows everything, sees everything and can control everything and everyone. If God truly possesses these qualities, why was any of it even necessary?

After many years of trials and tribulations, God's chosen people were shown a wonderful promised land and told not to worry that there were people already living there. Genocide would take care of that. And they nearly didn't get there. Numbers 16 tells how God lost his temper again and nearly wiped out the Israelites he had brought from Egypt. Thankfully, Aaron stopped God's deliberate genocidal plague with some incense, which was nice.

Later still, God wanted to forgive mankind for its sins, but for some reason he couldn't just say, "as long as you're good from now on, you are forgiven", he had to send his own son to be killed in a brutal way. But it wasn't really a sacrifice because he came back to life and this allowed people to start up a new way to worship the same God. And now there was a new element, eternal damnation and torture in hell.

We move on 600 years and once again God chooses another lowly soul, in an obscure desert location. This time there is the dictation of a book and the beginning of a new religion to supersede the others. This time it was to be the very last testament and would be spread by the sword, with its followers told to kill, lie, oppress and do whatever may be necessary to spread the new faith to the whole world. Every human would be given a choice; become Muslim, be a slave or die.

And finally, we reach the present day, where billions of people worship what they claim to be the same God but in ways so different that they must kill each other to ensure God only receives the right form of obedience. And God, who apparently loves us, allows and encourages this.

So, even if the highly implausible entity called God really exits, he is clearly not 'good' and certainly should not be worshipped. Religion is dangerous and belief can cause irrational and devastating behaviour.
Isn't it time we said, "enough is enough" and left all this superstition behind?

It's a brave new world. But only if we make it so. We have space exploration, the internet, modern medicine and rock music. Do we really want to be dictated to by our ancestors, who thought the world was a flat disc, stood on pillars, that outer space was filled with water, that disease was caused by evil spirits and who were eagerly waiting for God to end it all?

WHAT IS FAITH?

To many of us, this seems like a foolish question. Surely faith is the act of believing without evidence? Maybe but maybe not.

In the continual debate between the religious and the non-religious, the definition of faith has become a battleground. Non-believers, like me, offer a dictionary definition of the word as it is commonly used and in doing so we make an assertion that faith and facts are not the same. We state that whilst it is perfectly valid to have one's own beliefs, if those beliefs cannot be proven to be true, that is in accordance with reality, by use of evidence, then to assert them as true is to lie.
To repeat; faith and facts are not the same. Beliefs and knowledge are not the same.

But now we come to a problem. Christians, it seems, have invented their own definition of the word that is different to the way it is used by everyone else. Christian faith is not, apparently, believing without evidence but something far deeper. In order to try to understand this strange new definition, I have copied and pasted below a section from a website, 'christianityetc.org'

What is Christian Faith?

Definition
The Christian faith is the experience of daily living in a dynamic and new personal relationship with God through a transplanted "heart" of godly passions and emotions and a renewed "mind" of godly thoughts and wise Spirit directed personal choices. The key to this new experience of living, and its essential factor, is trusting God to make you into a new person by repenting of your arrogant selfish will choices and allowing him to place the Spirit on behalf of Jesus, his Son, into your heart and mind where Jesus (really Jesus, the Spirit, and God, the Father) can do their work to give you a new life of service for the glory of God.
I will freely admit that it took a couple of readings for me to understand what is being said here but I think the gist of it is the following: Christian faith is a number of separate but linked

things. It is trust in God and in his ability to change our old self into a new and better self. It is a daily practice of experiencing or feeling our relationship with God. And it is the hope that he will change us to make us willing subjects working for the glory of God. I hope I have that right.

There is an immediate problem here which should be apparent to anyone. Even if we accept the right of Christians to redefine a word for their own purpose, their position presupposes the existence of God. Something which cannot be proven and therefore must be taken on faith, in the old and commonly used sense.

So, what we have is not a fresh definition, it is merely an extension of the old which still rests upon the standard usage. Christians may like to read more into the word than the rest of us but, at its core, Christianity still requires an unproven belief in an immaterial, invisible, omniscient, omnipotent deity, which exists outside of our reality and which therefore cannot be proven to exist.

Like it or not Christians, faith retains its old definition and you use it in that way every day. Please stop pretending otherwise to try to win arguments by deflecting.

AFTERWORD

I have genuinely enjoyed putting this collection together and editing it to ensure it makes sense. I fully expect to be the next J K Rowling, judiciously mixed with a touch of Stephen Fry and to shortly be rolling in loot.

I have more essays to collate into a second book; lots more. Whether I do so will depend upon quite how wealthy I become. Fairly rich will encourage greater effort but obscenely rich will probably mean I will be too busy to bother.

I sincerely hope you enjoyed this book. I hope it made you think and even prompted you to consider doing something similar.

ABOUT THE AUTHOR

Paul Davis-Cooke

As a 63 year old Englishman of middling education and fairly progressive views, the author is not, at first glance, special. Or at second glance.

He has always enjoyed the sound of his own voice and has to be physically retrained from expounding on any subject at all.

He has had plenty of time to write this tome because he has few friends due to his boring obsession with the book's subject matter.